Outdoor Wood Projects

24 Projects You Can Build in a Weekend

Outdoor Wood Projects

24 Projects You Can Build in a Weekend

Steve Cory

The Taunton Press

The Taunton Press
Inspiration for hands-on living®

The Taunton Press, Inc., 63 South Main Street,
PO Box 5506, Newtown, CT 06470-5506
e-mail: tp@taunton.com

Editor: Christina Glennon
Copy editor: Seth Reichgott
Indexer: Jay Kreider
Jacket/Cover design: Jean-Marc Troadec
Interior design and layout: Tinsley Morrison
Illustrator: Mike Wanke
Photographer: Steve Cory

The following names/manufacturers appearing in *Outdoor Wood Projects* are trademarks:
IKEA®, Pau Lope®, Velcro®

Library of Congress Cataloging-in-Publication Data
Cory, Steve.
  Outdoor wood projects : 24 projects you can build in a weekend / Steve
Cory.
      pages cm
  ISBN 978-1-62113-808-2 (paperback)
  1. Woodworking--Amateurs' manuals. 2. Garden ornaments and furniture.
  3. Plant containers. I. Title.
  TT185.C74 2014
  684'.08--dc23
                                    2013050910

Printed in the United States of America
10 9 8 7 6 5 4 3 2 1

About Your Safety: Homebuilding is inherently dangerous. From accidents with power tools to falls from ladders, scaffolds, and roofs, builders risk serious injury and even death. We try to promote safe work habits through our books. But what is safe for one person under certain circumstances may not be safe for you under different circumstances. So don't try anything you learn about here (or elsewhere) unless you're certain that it is safe for you. Please be careful.

Acknowledgments

I THANK Bill West for his great ideas and unflagging energy in bringing many of these projects to reality. Diane Slavik, my lovely wife, provided much-needed photo and text assistance. Rosalie Ross Sennett, Leslie Tom, and David Ross gave greatly appreciated advice on working with bamboo. Rosalie's wonderful San Francisco patio is the setting for most of the bamboo photos. The IKEA® company provided parquet decking (the Platta series) that serves as the floor for some of the beauty shots. The Kreg company (www.kregtool.com) supplied tools for making pocket-screw joints. Christine Vollmer and Conrad Wennerberg, as well as Loren Santow, supplied yard spaces seen in many of the shots, not to mention liquid refreshments after long hot days of shooting. Next-door neighbors Arcilla and George Stahl graciously put up with all that noise and mess. And let's not forget Eleanor Cory, Alex Cory, and Dr. Nzube Okonkwo, hand models extraordinaire.

And many thanks to the staff members at The Taunton Press, Peter Chapman, Christina Glennon, and Erin Giunta, for patient and skillful editing and organizing.

contents

introduction

NOTHING QUITE EQUALS the satisfaction of building a project that adds charm and personality to your yard. If it is a memorable design and built well, even a small planter, trellis, or other feature will be a nice touch that makes your outdoor space more of a pleasure to use. Special details that complement the house or landscape can help to unify your outdoor space. A home-made project tailored to your space can tie it all together, adding your personal signature in a satisfying way. Who knows? Maybe one day your project may become a treasured heirloom.

Natural wood (and bamboo, though it is technically a grass) is the ideal material for a modest do-it-yourself project. Whether stained or left alone to turn a weathered gray, your new structure will effortlessly harmonize with leafy plants, colorful flowers, and nearby stone or brick surfaces. You also have the option of painting it a muted tone that barely asserts itself, or with bright colors that proudly announce its presence and make your yard a more whimsical place.

Working with wood is a pleasure with timeless appeal, as long as you approach it in the right way. Reserve ample space for construction, and do most of the work on a flat patio or deck surface, on a board-and-sawhorse table, or on a shop table. Most of these projects can be built indoors, though you may prefer working outdoors, where you can enjoy your surroundings and won't need to worry about the dust. We'll help you select tools and materials that make it easy to cut straight lines, create tight joints, and drive long-lasting fasteners.

We'll also help you choose the right wood—wood that will last for a long time and will have the look you want. This sometimes means spending more for high-quality cedar, redwood, ipé, or even top-rated treated wood. Or, if you are after a more rustic look, more inexpensive options such as pallet wood have the worn and weathered appeal of reclaimed or recycled materials.

The projects in this book are within the reach of a homeowner with modest skills and some basic tools. Still, we've chosen sophisticated designs that add flair, rather than boxy objects that shout "beginner." Most can be accomplished in less than a day, but are stylish enough to keep for a lifetime.

At a home center, landscape supply store, or garden center you may find wood products similar to those shown in this book, such as planters, trellises, and furniture. You may be tempted to outfit your yard with ready-made products. But take a closer look: Many of these planters, trellises, and furniture pieces are made with thin, flimsy wood and are joined with less-than-secure staples; if you grab the pieces and wiggle, you may find yourself less than confident in their durability. Many of these products have a cookie-cutter design that will give your patio or yard a ho-hum seen-that-before feel. And given the limited number of options, you may not be able to find a feature that neatly fits your space, or that feels at home with other parts of your landscape. Building yourself lets you craft features that are more elegant looking, better tailored to your needs, and more interesting and original.

The first chapter of this book will prepare you for the projects that follow. We'll show you how to choose wood and fasteners, we'll talk about the

tools you will need, and we'll also demonstrate basic techniques. The remaining chapters feature specific projects organized by category: planters, trellises, furniture, bamboo, and garden structures. In each chapter there are between three and seven projects with complete step-by-step instructions. We've also added a few project variations with general instructions. Using the information in this book together with just a little ingenuity, you will be able to build them all.

1

materials, tools & techniques

THE PROJECTS in this book tend to be modest, and most can be built using inexpensive lumber, simple screws or nails, and a circular saw or even a handsaw. But often even a minor budget increase or an hour or so of practice can result in finished products that look great and stay looking that way for a long time.

For instance, lesser grades of wood may have high moisture content, which means they will shrink, creating unsightly gaps in your joints as well as warping and cracking. This chapter explains how to choose boards that will retain their good looks and strength. We'll also cover fastening materials that hold more securely and look better than standard nails and screws.

If you have a standard handyman-type set of tools, including, say, a circular saw and hand miter box, you can build most of these projects. But to make the jobs go more smoothly and to produce cleaner-looking results, you may want to spend a few bucks on a minor upgrade, like a pocket-screw jig, a straight-hole attachment for a drill, or a better-quality hand miter box. Or you may choose to spend more for tools that make you feel like a pro, such as a power miter saw or a tablesaw.

No matter which tools you use, you can probably get better results by learning and employing tried-and-true building methods. Most of these techniques can be learned quickly, and will increase building time by only minutes, but can be the difference between an obviously amateur product and one that looks like it was made in a wood shop.

Choosing Wood

Despite the increasing popularity of vinyl and composite materials for outdoor structures, the natural beauty of wood resonates with most of us. Synthetics just can't rival the one-of-a-kind grain pattern found on each board of real wood. Wood surfaces—even if they are a bit cracked or warped—have their own special warmth and appeal and make an outdoor space feel more like a pleasant escape from the workaday world.

Still, while we may not need perfection, we do want boards that will retain their initial appearance without obvious blemishes. Too many planters and trellises start to look shabby after only a few years. Choosing the right lumber and perhaps applying a quick coat of finish every year or so will keep that from happening.

Wood Species and Types

Building an outdoor project out of untreated pine, fir, or hem-fir is possible, but wet rot will almost certainly occur unless you apply copious amounts of preservative, primer, and paint or stain and keep

WOOD SIZES

If you're new to working with wood, you may be surprised to find that a 2×4 is actually only 1½ in. by 3½ in. This is not really a sign of the decay of civilization: "Actual" sizes of boards have stayed pretty much the same since World War II. (Older full-size boards were rough-surfaced. At least to a certain extent, the smaller modern size is the result of planing, which smoothes the boards without significantly reducing strength.)

One-by lumber is ¾ in. thick; 2-bys are 1½ in. thick; and 4-bys are 3½ in. thick. Decking boards labeled "5/4" are exactly 1 in. thick.

The second number in a board's size is less predictable. A 1×4 or 2×4 is almost always exactly 3½ in. wide, but a 1×6 or 2×6 may be as much as ⅛ in. narrower or wider than 5½ in. Similarly, 1×8s or 2×8s are around 7¼ in. wide; 1×10s or 2×10s are around 9¼ in. wide. Sometimes boards from the same lumberyard stack vary significantly in width.

These boards are both 1×8, but vary significantly in width.

Many cedar and redwood boards contain both dark heartwood and lighter-colored sapwood.

Rough-sawn cedar is pretty much what its name promises, with a pleasingly furry skin.

the wood coated with religious zeal. The species we recommend have natural resistance to rot, though most of them still work better if kept sealed.

CEDAR AND REDWOOD

Western red cedar is available for reasonable prices in most parts of the country. (Other types, such as eastern white, incense, and northern white, are only locally available.) It is fairly soft—you can often dent it by pushing hard with your thumbnail—but hard enough to be used for decking. It's somewhat prone to cracking, but this is usually not a problem if you select boards carefully and drill pilot holes before driving fasteners near board ends. Its dark-colored heartwood is very resistant to rot, but the lighter-colored sapwood is less so. If possible, choose the dark boards. Still, cedar should be stained and sealed to keep it from rotting.

There are a good number of possible cedar grades. Look for words like "heart" and "tight knot." The top-end cedar, "clear heart," has no knots and is quite expensive. Boards labeled "S4S" are smooth on all four sides, while other boards may be rough on one side.

Boards labeled "5/4 decking" are 1 in. thick and 5½ in. wide. These can be an ideal and inexpensive choice for many projects. They have rounded edges that will create highly visible lines when two boards are butted together.

Redwood can be purchased in much of the country. If your lumberyard does not stock it, they can probably order it. It is extremely stable and resistant to cracking, and fairly hard, making it superior to cedar; but it is usually also more expensive. As with cedar, the dark heartwood will resist rot much better than the lighter sapwood.

There are many possible redwood grades, though your local supplier will probably stock only a few at most. Those that include the word "common" have at least some sapwood; various "heart" or "all heart"

GOING GRAY?

All the woods described on these pages—cedar, redwood, ironwood, and treated—can be stained regularly, or can be left alone and allowed to "go gray." The gray that you get will vary, depending on the wood. High-grade redwood and ironwood turn a beautiful silvery gray with a subtle sheen. Treated lumber, on the other hand, may turn a gray that would be better described as "muddy." The gray tone of cedar and lesser redwood grades is somewhere between, and may please some people while looking sloppy to others. The advantage of going gray, of course, is low maintenance: You really don't have to do anything. There

are, however, disadvantages: Gone-gray wood is unprotected. That means that spills or splashes may create stains that are difficult to remove. And gray wood may dry out severely, especially in dry climates, which can lead to cracking and warping.

Unless it has cracked or warped, grayed wood can usually be restored and stained. Wash it with a pressure-washer, deck cleaner, wood bleach, or a solution of one part household bleach to two parts water, and rinse. Allow to dry completely, and perhaps repeat if the color is blotchy. Then apply the stain and sealer of your choice.

The grayed cedar shown at left has attractive silvery tones with interesting grain patterns. The grayed treated wood shown at right is far less easy on the eyes.

grades will be darker and longer lasting. The highest grade, Clear All Heart, is probably too pricey; Heart B has very few knots and is more affordable. For a pleasant knotty appearance and good rot resistance, perhaps choose Construction Heart or Merchantable Heart.

DOG-EARED FENCING

At a home center you can almost always find "dog-eared fencing," 6-ft.-long boards with small angles cut off the corners at one end. These tend to be ⅝ in. thick (though thickness varies) and 5½ in. wide. Dog-eared fencing is available as pressure-treated or cedar. The cedar is rough-surfaced, while the treated boards are fairly smooth.

Quality varies widely from board to board. Some will have visible splits and other imperfections like bowing or cupping (see p. 13). But sometimes you can find boards that are remarkably sound and good-looking. Choose boards that are light-weight over heavier boards, which retain a good deal of moisture and may crack when they dry out. Since they are thin, they won't be terribly strong, but will be strong enough for small containers and other projects. Also, their thinness sometimes requires extra care when driving fasteners. But carefully chosen boards look great, and you can't beat the price.

These stacks of cedar and pressure-treated dog-eared fencing are in better-than-average shape. As long as they are not heavy with moisture, they are likely to last a good long time with little cracking or warping.

IRONWOODS

Brazilian hardwoods, also called ironwoods, are the highest-priced natural wood option. The most common species is ipé, which is sometimes called Pau Lopé®. Ipé is extraordinarily hard (it even has a fire rating similar to metal) and impervious to rot. Other species go by a bewildering number of possible names, including garapa, cumaru, and tigerwood. All are very hard and rot resistant, but some are a bit softer and less expensive than ipé.

It may be worth your while to look into available options, because they vary in appearance. For instance, ipé is generally dark, with subtle color variations and close, dense grain; tigerwood has pronounced grain lines that vary greatly in width

Ironwood options include ipé/Pau Lopé (left) and cumaru (right).

Cutting ironwood calls for a hefty tablesaw or a chopsaw that has a sharp blade.

Pressure-treated boards have various colors and grain patterns. Here, one board has some light-green hues; another has very pronounced grain lines; and another has a mellow, pleasing tone.

and color; garapa tends toward a light, honey color; cumaru has a slightly reddish tint; and so on.

Because it's so hard, working with ironwood calls for good equipment: You'll need a power saw with a good carbide blade, and you'll need to predrill pilot holes before driving all the fasteners. This slows the project down, but is worth the extra effort.

Ironwood is usually available as 1×4, 2×4, 5/4×6, and 2×6. Local lumberyards may not have it in stock, but they should be able to order it.

You can allow ironwood to go gray, but after spending all that money most people choose to give the wood a quick application of stain/sealer once a year.

PRESSURE-TREATED LUMBER

Greenish or yellowish treated lumber is often used for underlying structures rather than for visible elements. But high-quality treated lumber can be a good choice for small projects. Treated boards are inexpensive and very resistant to rot.

In most parts of the country treated lumber is Southern yellow pine (SYP), a fairly hard wood that accepts the liquid treatment readily. In some areas fir or hem-fir is used instead. Douglas fir is very strong and stable, but it doesn't accept the treatment well, so it is incised with a pattern of slits (for injecting the treatment) and these slits will not fade away in time. "Hem-fir" can actually refer to a number of species. Some of them are stable and

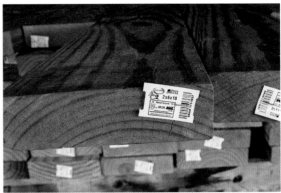

Treated lumber rated for above ground is fine for many purposes, but choose boards rated for ground contact if soil will touch them or if they will stay wet for long periods.

This board is rated no. 2 prime, so it is strong with no large knots or other serious flaws. "KD19" means it was kiln-dried, with a moisture content of 19 percent or less.

strong, while others are prone to shrinking, warping, and cracking. Consult with your lumber supplier to learn how well you can expect your hem-fir to perform.

Treated lumber can be made surprisingly attractive—in a rustic sort of way—if you apply the right stain and sealer. Stains made specifically for treated wood generally contain a bit more red tint, to overcome the boards' green or yellow appearance.

If your project will come into contact with soil, buy boards labeled "ground contact"; if it will not, you can use the less expensive boards rated for "above ground" use.

The highest quality treated lumber is often called KDAT, meaning kiln-dried after treatment. Other designations, such as "select" or "no. 1" also indicate high quality.

STAINED-AND-TREATED WOOD

Some lumberyards sell treated boards with a cedar-like color. These boards have the same rot-preventing treatment as the greenish boards, but with added color. They are most often available as 5/4 decking boards. The price is a bit higher than for greenish boards, partly because of the colorant and partly because no. 1 lumber is usually used.

Color varies from batch to batch and even from board to board, so choose boards individually. In some cases you may be pleased enough with the appearance to leave it alone after building. Or you may choose to apply a light stain to achieve the final desired color. Expect the color to fade in a couple of weeks, especially if the boards are exposed to direct sunlight. You will need to restain the boards after a year or two.

CAN YOU GROW VEGETABLES NEAR TREATED LUMBER?

Older treated lumber used CCA treatment, which contained arsenic, but CCA has been banned for a long time. The treated lumber you buy today has no arsenic, and the treatment is composed mostly of copper. There isn't any good evidence that soil coming into contact with treated lumber will transfer harmful chemicals to planted vegetables, but some people are still wary, and currently food labeled "organic" is not allowed to be grown near treated wood. If you are concerned, use another wood, or line the planter with plastic sheeting before adding soil.

Some composites are solid color, while others have color variations that mimic the look of natural wood.

At a pallet yard you will find tall stacks of pallets. The proprietors will likely give you a small number to choose among. They may have some stacks of decking boards already removed from the pallets.

COMPOSITES

Composite lumber is not natural wood, but it does contain wood fibers, so it merits a mention here. Composite decking and railing has exploded in popularity in many areas of the country. The better-quality composites are often just as expensive as ironwood. Their advantage is greatly lowered maintenance: The best composites will not change in appearance after decades of use, and need only be hosed or brushed off once in a while.

Be aware, however, that many lower-cost composites will fade in the sun, they may attract mildew or mold in damp conditions, and they may even warp. Check with local builders or people with composite decks to see which products stay beautiful for years in your climate.

PALLET WOOD

Sometimes a rustic, roughed-up look is just right for an outdoor project. And sometimes you want to build something out of dirt-cheap materials. Pallet wood may meet both of these goals.

In most cities and large towns you can find places that buy, store, and sell pallets, which are made to be toted around with a forklift. Some of these places will be happy to sell you pallets for a small price; others don't want to bother with people who just want a few pallets. Pallets are often left lying around in alleys or behind stores, where you may be able to scavenge them for free.

Pallets generally range in size from 36 in. by 36 in. to 48 in. by 48 in. Most have three 2-by stringers, which are notched to accommodate the forklift, making them useless for most projects. The deck boards are generally about $5/8$ in. thick. Many have a combination of wide and narrow deck boards. Newer-looking pallets are rated "A"; these may actually be too new-looking for your tastes. Less-expensive "B" pallets often have that nicely weathered look.

At a pallet yard you may find stacks of deck boards that have already been removed. I visited a yard in Chicago, where I was told to take as many of these as I wanted, for free.

Pallet boards are often pine, though it is not uncommon to see oak and other species. You can't count on pallet wood to stay rot-free for decades, but if you apply a good stain/sealer or paint they can last a good long time.

Moisture Content

Freshly cut lumber contains varying amounts of moisture. As the wood dries out, it will shrink, and it may also develop warping and cracking. Wood starts to dry out during the milling process; it will usually dry more while stored in the lumberyard; and, if it is still wet when you buy it, it will continue to dry after you have built your project. If wood is stored in humid or damp conditions, it may actually absorb moisture. Pressure-treated lumber has liquid treatment injected into it, and this also must dry out for a board to be stable.

In theory, a board's moisture content should reflect the ambient air humidity. But in practice, and in all but the most humid locales, you can follow a simple rule: The dryer the wood you buy, the fewer unpleasant surprises await you after building. To avoid warping and cracking, select boards that have a low moisture content. And the dryer your climate, the dryer your wood should be.

Many boards are simply air dried (sometimes indicated by AD on the stamp), but kiln-dried lumber is actually heated in a sort of oven. Kiln-dried lumber (with a stamp that says KD or KDAT) is more expensive, but usually better quality.

You can test the moisture content of a board simply by picking it up and comparing it to other boards of a similar size: The heavier the board, the wetter it is. You also may see a stamp indicating the moisture content (MC), expressed in a percentage. A stamp designation of S-DRY, meaning "surface dry," will have a low moisture content. Avoid boards that are over 20 percent (many are stamped with S-GRN, meaning "surface green"); boards under 12 percent are the most stable.

tip

You will have the best chance of finding great boards if you shop at a lumberyard or home center that takes good care of their wood. Boards should be laid flat; if they are stacked upright, they will almost certainly warp. The staff should keep the boards stacked tightly together, so they don't have a chance to crook, twist, or cup. And there should be a larger-than-average selection, so you can choose boards like high-quality cedar, redwood, and ipé.

These boards both have wide grain, so they are OK to use but not ideal. The one on the right is primarily vertical grain, making it preferable to the flat-grained board on the left.

These boards both have fairly tight, narrow grain. The board on the left also has vertical grain, making it more stable than the flat-grained one on the right.

Wood Grain

As a general rule, the narrower a board's grain pattern, the more stable the board will be. Ring width is a function of two factors. First, trees that grow quickly have wider rings. (As you may recall from grade school, each ring represents a year of

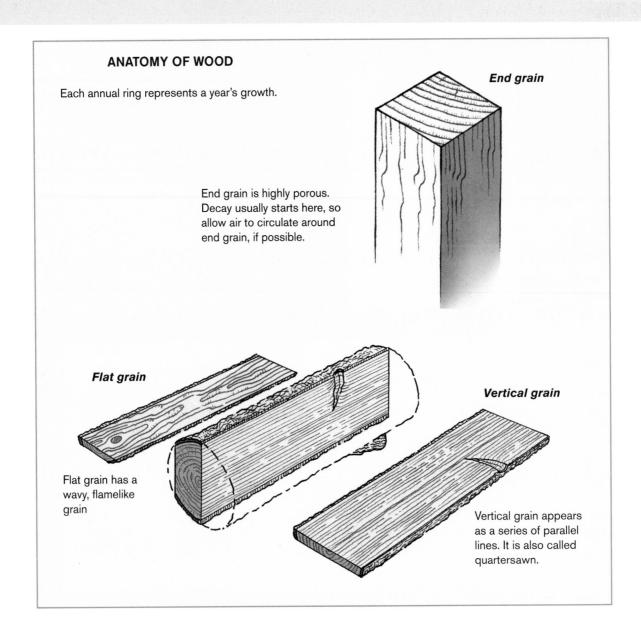

ANATOMY OF WOOD

Each annual ring represents a year's growth.

End grain

End grain is highly porous.
Decay usually starts here, so
allow air to circulate around
end grain, if possible.

Flat grain

Flat grain has a
wavy, flamelike
grain

Vertical grain

Vertical grain appears
as a series of parallel
lines. It is also called
quartersawn.

growth.) Trees with narrow growth rings are denser
and stronger.

Second, it matters where the board was cut from
the log (see the illustration above). Boards cut
perpendicular to the rings are often called quartersawn, and have vertical grain—a simple pattern of
closely-spaced grain lines. Boards cut parallel to
the rings have flat grain—a more varied pattern of
widely spaced, wavy lines. As you may expect, the
narrow-grained wood is less likely to warp.

Many boards have a combination of vertical and
flat grain; the more vertical grain, the better.

Avoiding Wood Defects

In addition to choosing the type of lumber to
use, take time to inspect and select each board.
Choose boards free of serious defects that could
cause problems in years to come.

For each board look at the face and edges that
will be visible. (Usually, one side will be hidden.)
Pay special attention to the ends, where damage
is most likely to appear. Then pick up one end and
sight along the length of the board, to see if it has
bends or twists. Here are some common defects to
watch for:

A quality lumberyard keeps boards tightly stacked and protected from the weather to minimize warpage.

CROOK OR BOW

If a board bends along its length but is otherwise flat, it has a crook. Few boards are perfectly straight. If the bend is only slight, that is called a bow—a common condition that can usually be straightened out as you build. A more serious crook, however, may be impossible to straighten, so choose another board.

TWIST

If a board has multiple bends, so it cannot lie flat, it is twisted. Twisted boards are difficult to straighten, so you should not buy one.

CUPPING

A board that is curved along its width is cupped. Very slight cupping can usually be corrected when you attach the board, but if the cupping is very noticeable, the board may crack when you use fasteners to flatten it.

KNOTS

If a knot is less than 1½ in. in diameter and tightly embedded in the board, it is a cosmetic rather than a structural matter. Knots can be pretty or ugly, depending on your point of view and your project goals. If a knot is large and you can see gaps between it and the rest of the board, it may well fall out in time, so move on to the next board unless you like the occasional knot hole.

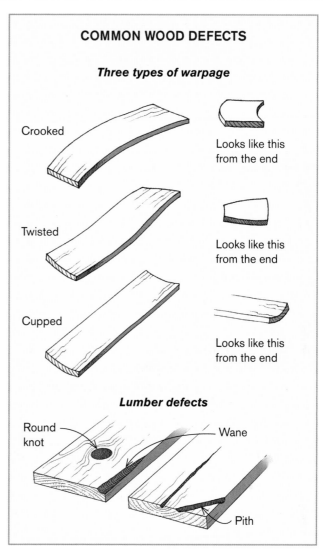

COMMON WOOD DEFECTS

Three types of warpage

Crooked

Looks like this from the end

Twisted

Looks like this from the end

Cupped

Looks like this from the end

Lumber defects

Round knot

Wane

Pith

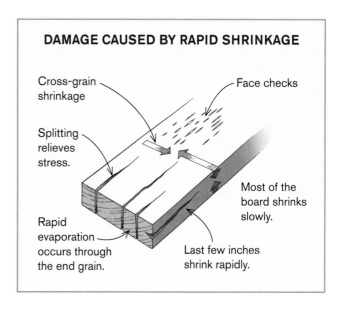

DAMAGE CAUSED BY RAPID SHRINKAGE

Cross-grain shrinkage

Face checks

Splitting relieves stress.

Most of the board shrinks slowly.

Rapid evaporation occurs through the end grain.

Last few inches shrink rapidly.

WANE

Wane refers to missing wood or visible bark, usually along a corner. Unless the wane is large, this is a cosmetic matter only, and you may be able to position the board so the wane is not visible when your project is built.

PITH

Pith is similar to wane, but is usually a narrow strip in the middle of a board. It may peel off once the board fully dries, so avoid using the board unless you can hide the pith.

CHECKING

Checking is a pattern of very shallow cracks on the face of a board. It is a cosmetic problem only—and some people actually like the look.

SPLITTING

Because a board often dries more rapidly at its ends, you may find splits there. Splits may grow longer with time. However, if your project allows you to cut the board to remove the splits plus an inch or more, then the board will probably be fine.

Sighting down this board's length shows that it has a very modest bow, making it straight enough for nearly all purposes.

Fasteners and Adhesives

Because most of the projects in this book are small, buying top-notch fasteners will not break your budget. You may choose fasteners that recede visually, or you may appreciate the look of large-headed fasteners, perhaps even with washers.

Avoid using fasteners designed for indoor use. "Common" or "box" nails, or "cement coated sinkers," will surely rust after a few rains, and they may react to the tannins in cedar or redwood, which will cause stains. Inexpensive screws labeled "all-purpose," "drywall," or even "gold" look fine when installed, but will also rust.

THE RIGHT LENGTH

Whether you are fastening with screws or nails, get fasteners of the right length. In general, a nail or screw should penetrate the receiving board—the board you are fastening to—by $1\frac{1}{2}$ in., perhaps a bit more. So, for instance, if you are attaching a 1-in.-thick board, use a nail or screw that is $2\frac{1}{2}$ in. long. If you are attaching a 2-by, which is $1\frac{1}{2}$ in. thick, use a 3-in. fastener. And if you will attach a 1-by, which is $\frac{3}{4}$ in. thick, use $2\frac{1}{4}$-in. fasteners. The exception: In some projects, a too-long fastener will poke through and its point will be visible. In that case, measure carefully so that the fastener will penetrate most, but not all, of the receiving board.

Stainless-steel screws are excellent fasteners. Be sure to drive them with a bit that fits tightly—usually a #1 square-drive.

Coated deck screws come in a variety of colors and head types.

Galvanized nails are another option. The twist-screw nails at right will hold firmer than the straight box nails at left.

These self-piloting screws have a tip that drills a hole as they drive, so you do not need to predrill pilot holes.

SCREWS

Nowadays you can drive screws just as fast as nails. Screws hold more securely than nails. And if you make a mistake, it is much easier to remove screws than to remove nails, so you can some-times correct an error without visible damage. See pp. 28–29 for tips on driving screws.

Stainless-steel screws These are sure to last, are extremely strong, and are absolutely guaran-teed not to rust. They are somewhat expensive, but for a modest-size project they'll probably only add a few dollars to the materials cost. Most stainless-steel screws sold today have small heads, and many are square-drive.

Deck screws Screws specifically made for fastening decking are typically coated with a thick weather-resistant finish that virtually eliminates the possibility of rust. Most types are also very strong, and they are not as expensive as stainless steel.

As a bonus, deck screws come in several colors, so their heads may virtually disappear once you have stained your project. Deck screws may be Phillips, square-drive, or driveable only by using a screw-driver bit supplied by the manufacturer.

Galvanized Simple galvanized screws are inex-pensive, but do not reliably guarantee against rust. Unless you live in a dry climate where rust is not a problem, they are not recommended.

Self-piloting screws It's a very good idea to drill a pilot hole before driving most screws to prevent cracking the board. Some deck screws however, have tips configured like a drill bit, so they actually bore their own pilot holes as you drive them. This can save time and aggravation. A downside is that they are usually difficult to remove if you make a mistake.

Wood glue and polyurethane glue can be bought in small squeeze bottles.

Construction adhesives are applied with a caulk gun.

NAILS

Nails are not as strong as screws, but they do hold tight if you use the right kind and size—and if you drive them accurately. Also, many people prefer the classic look of a simple, round nail head over a screw head. Use galvanized nails; their heads are generally much less likely to rust than galvanized screw heads.

ADHESIVES

A quality adhesive, if applied correctly, can be very strong—in some cases, stronger than the wood fibers themselves. Usually you will use adhesives along with screws, nails, dowels, or other fasteners. Applying an adhesive will allow you to install fewer fasteners. There are a number of options for adhering outdoor projects.

Wood glue Wood glue is easy to apply and provides good adhesion. Choose a glue specifically designed for outdoor use, rather than an all-purpose glue. Apply a thin coat to one or both surfaces to be joined, then attach with fasteners. You may need to wipe away squeezed-out glue using a damp cloth, which is easy to do.

Polyurethane glue This also comes in squeeze bottles rather than caulk tubes. Polyurethane glue reacts to moisture, so it is common practice to lightly spray or wipe both surfaces with a small amount of water before applying. Once applied, the glue will slowly foam up; you will need to wait at least an hour, then sand or cut off the dried foam. Many woodworkers feel that poly glue is so strong that it is worth this extra trouble.

Construction adhesive A variety of construction adhesives are available in caulking tubes, and you may choose to use one on a larger project. Be sure to use an adhesive specifically rated for outdoor use. In general, better adhesives cost a bit more. If you plan to paint the project, consider an "adhesive caulk," which will both seal and adhere. The strongest type is a polyurethane adhesive: It will foam up a bit, like polyurethane glue. The more-expensive "professional" grade is the strongest of all.

> **tip**
> Some cheap tape measures have inches on one side and centimeters on the other. This may seem like a good idea, but actually it tends to drive people a bit nuts, since they have to ignore half of the markings.

A 1-in.-wide tape measure is the only measuring tool most people need.

Measuring and Marking

Sometimes tired old sayings are true, and none is truer than "Measure twice and cut once." It's surprisingly easy to make measuring mistakes, and once cut, a board cannot be lengthened. So remove any distractions, disabuse yourself of the illusion that you can "multitask," and take your sweet time to be absolutely sure you've measured correctly before you pick up that saw.

MEASURING

Get a good tape measure with clearly visible lines. Though the projects in this book rarely call for long boards, get a large tape measure with a 1-in.-wide tape, because it is more stable and the markings are easier to read.

To help ensure against measuring mistakes, write the dimension on paper or a scrap board, or at least speak it out loud.

If a measurement is in sixteenths (for example, $5^{7}/_{16}$ in.), it's time-consuming to try to figure out the fraction's number. Many carpenters use "plus" and "minus" to indicate $1/_{16}$ in. more or less than the nearest $1/_2$ in. or $1/_4$ in. For example, instead of saying or writing "five and seven sixteenths," say or write "five and one-half minus"; for $5^{9}/_{16}$ in., use "five and one half plus." Another method is to "cut

tip

A tape measure's hook slides back and forth by about $1/_8$ in.—which is the thickness of the hook. Don't make the mistake of crimping the hook to keep it stable. It slides so you will get accurate measurements whether hooking it onto a board's end or butting against an adjacent surface. If a hook gets bent or otherwise damaged, buy another tape measure; using a damaged one will only lead to inaccurate measurements.

the line" (cut so as to completely eliminate the pencil line) in order to subtract $1/_{16}$ in. and "leave the line" to add a sixteenth.

You may be tempted to use a framing square or a level with inch markings, but you'll have to take special care to hold the tool perfectly aligned with the board's end. Use a good tape measure instead.

tip

Outdoor projects rarely need to get more exact than $1/_{16}$th of an inch. Some tape measures have, over their first few inches, little lines indicating 32ds of an inch. Most people find these useless, so you can probably ignore these little lines.

Use an angle square and a carpenter's square often, to maintain neat-looking right angles on your projects.

You can use a utility knife to sharpen a carpenter's pencil, but a regular pencil sharpener works better for a standard pencil.

MARKING A BOARD FOR CUTTING TO LENGTH

A carpenter's pencil has a wide, flat lead that lasts longer than a standard pencil, and is a good choice for construction projects. For smaller projects a standard pencil may be a better option, because it makes a finer line. Keep a sharpener on hand, and use it often.

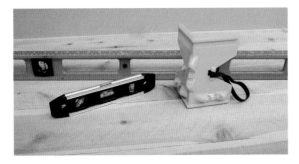

A short torpedo level and a longer carpenter's level help you quickly check for level and plumb. A post level makes it easy to keep posts plumb while you work.

CHECKING FOR SQUARE, LEVEL, AND PLUMB

Most projects need to be continually checked for square to ensure that corners are at perfect 90-degree angles. For very small projects an angle square (also called a speed square) works fine. An angle square is also handy for marking boards and as a guide for making square cuts with a circular saw. For greater accuracy, especially for larger projects, use a framing square.

Projects that are anchored to the ground need to have boards that are plumb (perpendicular to the earth) and level (parallel to the earth). A carpenter's level works fine for this. To check a post for plumb hands-free, strap on a post level, which will check for plumb in both directions at once.

> **tip**
>
> Check that your level is accurate: Place it on a level or near-level surface and look at the bubble. Flip it over and look at the bubble again. If it has moved, then the bubble vial is misaligned. Do the same on a plumb or near-plumb surface. If the bubble moves and you cannot adjust the vial, get a new level.

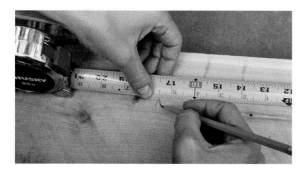

1 Mark a board for cutting by marking a V, with the point of the V indicating the exact dimension.

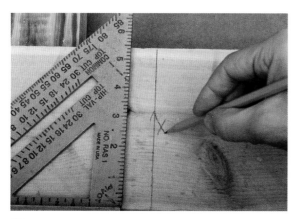

3 To ensure that you cut the correct side of the line, mark an X on the waste side. (If you will use the waste side for another piece, you may want to skip this step, so you don't have a lot of erasing to do.)

tip

Some carpenters prefer to make their marks using a utility knife instead of a pencil, because it makes a more precise line. Also, if you cut alongside the knife line, there is less chance of chipping the wood.

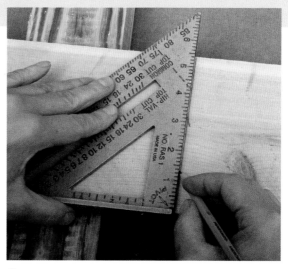

2 Hold the pencil tip on the tip of the V, and slide an angle square against it. Hold the square firmly against the board as you use it as a guide to draw a cut line through the V.

OTHER MARKING TOOLS

To mark a straight line you can use a carpenter's level or other straightedge. For a long line, use a chalkline. Fill the chalkline with chalk that is blue or another washable color; red chalk is permanent.

If your project includes an odd angle (not 45 or 90 degrees) that repeats, use a T bevel: Position the handle and the blade against the adjacent surfaces and tighten the nut. Now you can use it to mark other boards at the same angle.

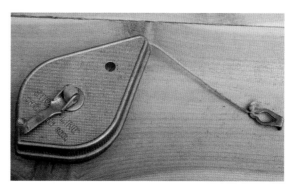

A chalkline is an inexpensive tool that quickly marks perfectly straight lines.

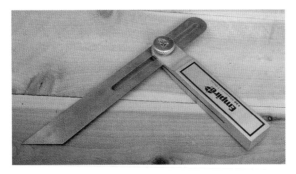

A T bevel has an adjustable blade that allows you to capture and recreate odd angles.

Hand Tools for Cutting and Shaping

Though you may spend most of your time working with power tools, you will need a basic set of hand tools as well. (For hand sanding blocks, see p. 43.)

HAND MITER SAW

If you're an old-fashioned kind of person or just on a budget, you may choose to cut boards using an old-fashioned handsaw. The advantage of a handsaw is that it doesn't throw off sawdust, so you can use it indoors. But unless you are in practice, a simple handsaw is difficult to use. A better-quality hand miter saw can often handle boards as large as 2×6, as long as the wood is soft. An even better option is to use a good miter box that features a thin, sharp blade kept rigid by a metal frame. It will slide up and down on two metal posts, for straight cuts. It should have stops for 90, 45, and 22½-degree cuts. A better model will have a clamping feature that holds the board tight while you cut.

A retractable utility knife (left) hides the blade when not in use. If you prefer a fixed-blade knife (right), be sure to store it where you will not accidentally cut yourself.

Armed with a couple of small chisels, a small plane, and a surform tool, you will be ready to make quick modifications to boards.

A good hand miter saw with a sharp blade can cut through cedar and other soft woods with relative ease and precision.

> **tip**
> If a plane sticks when pushed, it may need to be adjusted for a thinner cut, or you may need to run it in the opposite direction on the board.

CLAMPS

You may sometimes find that you need to hold pieces together while working on them. You could ask a friend or spouse to assist, but a good clamp usually does a better job. Small squeeze clamps are simple spring devices, much like large clothespins; they have minimal holding power, but often come in handy. Other small clamps ratchet down for a tighter grip. Bar clamps have longer reach. Some of these tighten by twisting a screw handle, while others tighten by squeezing a handle. Pipe clamps are inexpensive and versatile; they can be as long as the pipe you attach them to. A corner clamp holds pieces at a 90-degree angle.

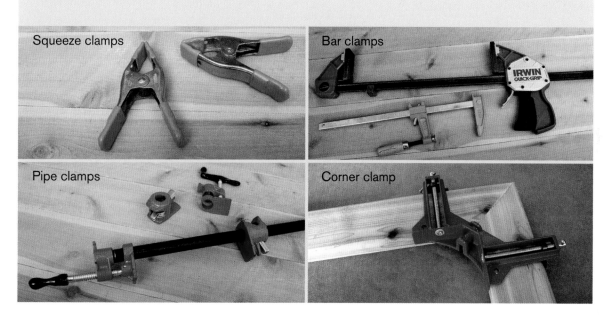

Squeeze clamps

Bar clamps

Pipe clamps

Corner clamp

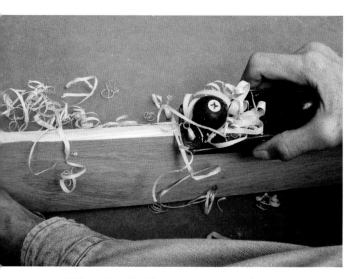

If the plane's blade is sharp and it is adjusted to just the right thickness, planing should proceed smoothly, with only moderate pressure required.

SHAPING TOOLS

After cutting a board you may need to use a utility knife to remove little burrs. It can also be useful for opening products and breaking plastic bands holding boards together. You'll occasionally use a chisel to finish cutouts and to make small modifications to a board. Keep yours sharp, and avoid using it for demolition work.

Use a wood plane to shave board edges and to smooth out rough spots. It takes a bit of patience at first to adjust its blade to just the right thickness, but once you've got it right it can be downright fun to watch the paper-thin curlicued strips of wood snake their way through the plane as you work. Nowadays many people use a surform tool instead, because it doesn't need adjusting or call for any skill. It will shave the board, but will leave a less-than-smooth surface behind.

Circular Saw

If used carefully, a circular saw can makes cross-cuts, ripcuts, and angled cuts that are as accurate as you need for most outdoor projects. Many of the instructions in this book show cutting with a tablesaw or power miter saw, but in most cases you could use a circular saw instead.

CHOOSING A CIRCULAR SAW

A standard corded circular saw has a 7 1/4-in. blade. This allows it to cut through 2-by lumber at a 45-degree bevel—all the cutting depth you need for most projects. (If you need to cut through a 4-by, you will need to make two passes.)

Check the specs. A good-quality circular saw will be rated at 12 amps or more. It will have ball bearings or roller bearings rather than sleeve bearings. Its base plate (the part that rests on the wood) should be made of cast metal, preferably with reinforcing ribs; cheaper aluminum base plates may bend out of true.

The saw should feel solid and comfortable in your hand. Check that you can smoothly adjust the depth of cut, and also the bevel. The adjust-

A good mid-priced circular saw will feel solid and cut cleanly.

Check the bevel adjustment (bottom), which determines the angle at which the blade crosses the board, as well as the depth adjustment (top). Both should be easy to adjust and easy to tighten.

> **tip**
>
> A "crosscut" is a cut made perpendicular to a board's length; it cuts the board to the desired length. A "ripcut" is made parallel to a board's length; it cuts a board to the desired width.

ment handles should be large and easy to loosen and tighten. The markings for the angles should be easy to read. Also check the sight lines: When cutting, you should have a clear view of the blade to be sure you are cutting alongside the line.

Features to look for An "anti-snag" guard will keep the guard from getting stuck when you cut at an angle, or when you cut near the end of a board—two common and very annoying problems. Some saws have a clearly readable gauge that tells you how deep the blade is set to cut. And some have laser lights that help guide your cut.

A GOOD BLADE

In the past carpenters often changed blades depending on whether they wanted a rough or fine cut, or whether they were cross- or rip-cutting. Nowadays many high-quality all-purpose blades can make clean cuts and last a long time. The rule to remember is this: The larger the number of teeth, the cleaner the cut. I recommend a carbide-tipped blade with 40 or more teeth.

A blade made for finish work is the best choice for most small projects. It will cut cleanly, with minimal "tearout"—the ragged edge on the top or bottom of the board you are cutting created by a dull or rough-cut blade. If you have lots of treated 2-by lumber to cut, or if you need to cut ipé or other hardwood, switch to a heavier duty blade.

If cutting becomes noticeably more difficult, it's time to change sawblades. A dull blade makes it difficult to produce straight cuts and creates unsightly tearout.

CHECKING THE BLADE FOR SQUARE

It's important that you make most cuts at a true 90-degree bevel; otherwise pieces placed side by side (as often happens in our projects) will not look neat. Just because the saw's guide says "90 degrees" does not guarantee that it is truly perpendicular to the base plate. Unplug the saw, adjust the blade to full depth, and turn it upside down. Hold an angle square against the base plate and the blade and check for square (p. 25).

A high-quality finishing blade with plenty of carbide-tipped teeth will make crisp cuts in thin wood and will also handle cutting of 2-by treated or hardwood lumber without dulling too quickly.

safety tip

Though commonly used by homeowners, a circular saw is a serious cutting tool that can do serious damage to the human body. Follow safety precautions: Unplug the saw before making adjustments or changing a blade. Do not modify the blade guard, even if it seems in the way; it should always be operating to protect you from the spinning blade. Support the board being cut, as shown on p. 24. Wear safety glasses when cutting, so splinters do not damage your eyes.

SUPPORT THE BOARD YOU'RE CUTTING

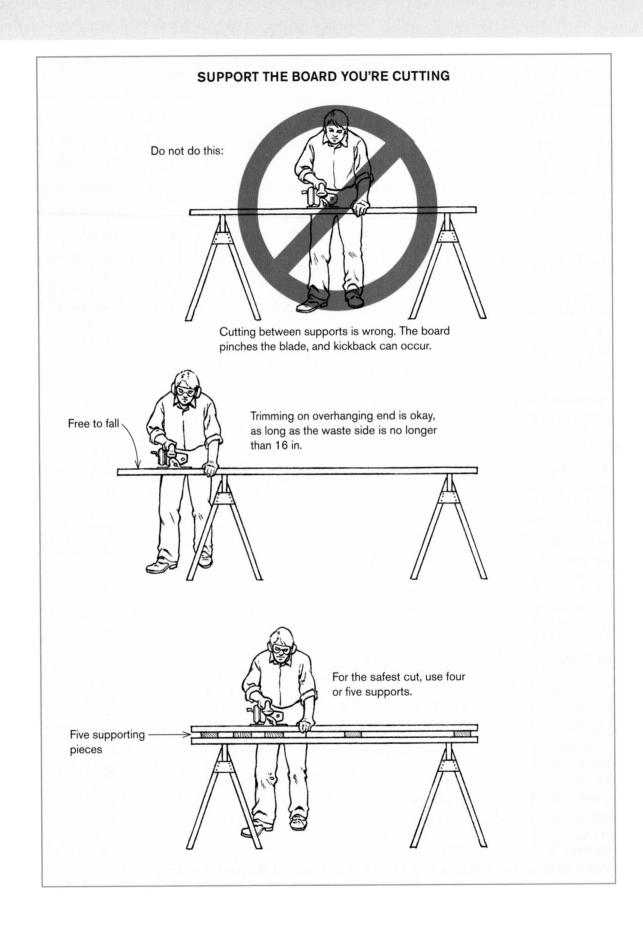

Do not do this:

Cutting between supports is wrong. The board pinches the blade, and kickback can occur.

Free to fall

Trimming on overhanging end is okay, as long as the waste side is no longer than 16 in.

For the safest cut, use four or five supports.

Five supporting pieces

A more accurate test: Cut through a board. Flip one of the cut pieces over and butt the two ends against each other. The cuts should be perfectly parallel.

If your blade is out of square, some saws allow you to adjust the guide so it will be perfectly square whenever you adjust it to 90 degrees. Others do not have this option, so you may need to micro-adjust the blade every time you change the bevel.

SUPPORT THE WORK TO AVOID KICKBACK AND SPLINTERING

It's very important to correctly support the board being cut to prevent one of two very bad things: (1) If a long section of the board is left unsupported on one side of the cut, it will start to fall before the cut is finished, which can lead to a splintered end and a ruined cut. (2) More dangerously, if a board is cut in its middle, with no support on the sides (top illustration on the facing page), it will bend down and pinch the blade, which can cause the saw to kick back at you.

If the waste side of the cut will be short—say, less than 16 in.—it will be light enough so it can hang unsupported, as shown in the middle drawing on the facing page. It will fall away when the cut is completed.

If the cut will be in the middle of a board, use board scraps to support it in four or five places, as shown in the bottom drawing on the facing page. That way, when the cut is completed both sides will stay in place.

USING THE SAW

With the saw unplugged, adjust the depth of the blade so it is about two thirds of a sawtooth's depth below the bottom of the board—about 1/4 in. This makes for a cleaner cut on the underside of the board.

With practice you can make accurate freehand cuts. But for greater accuracy use an angle square as a guide. Turn the saw on and push the saw until the blade touches the cut line. Slide the angle square against the base plate, grip the square firmly,

Unplug the saw and check it for square before making cuts.

> **tip**
>
> Cordless circular saws are more powerful than they used to be, and they work well for cutting 1-by and 5/4 lumber, especially if it is cedar or another softwood. However, if you need to cut hardwood or lots of treated wood you may find it lacking in power. A cordless circular saw will likely use a 6½-in. blade, which makes it capable of cutting through 2-by lumber at 90 degrees, but not at a 45-degree bevel.

and make the cut with the base plate pressed against the square.

To make an accurate ripcut, start by cutting an inch or so freehand. Then slide the rip guide against the board and tighten the setscrew to hold it in place. Finish the cut with the rip guide pressed against the edge of the board.

Set the blade so it is about ¼ in. deeper than the thickness of the board.

Hold an angle square firmly in place to guide a crosscut.

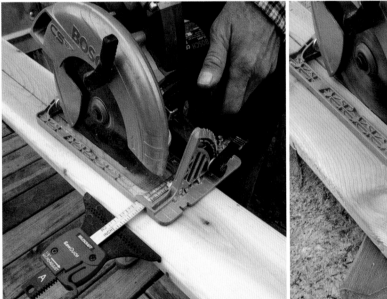

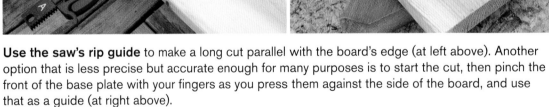

Use the saw's rip guide to make a long cut parallel with the board's edge (at left above). Another option that is less precise but accurate enough for many purposes is to start the cut, then pinch the front of the base plate with your fingers as you press them against the side of the board, and use that as a guide (at right above).

Jigsaw

Also called a saber saw, a jigsaw cuts curves with relative ease. Choose a model rated at 5 amps or more. The blade should be seated in a bearing guide that keeps it from wandering. A model with elliptical blade motion, rather than a straight up-and-down motion, gives you better control.

A cheap jigsaw has a base plate that is hard to tighten, making it difficult to maintain a cut that is perpendicular to the face of the board. A better jigsaw will hold the blade firmly perpendicular to the base plate for more professional results.

Buy a variety of blades for different purposes. You'll need narrow, small-toothed blades for tight curves on 1-by lumber. For cutting 2-by lumber, use a wider blade with coarser teeth. Blades can go dull quickly; change yours when the cutting gets laborious or when it produces ragged edges.

Cutting with a jigsaw takes a knack (you always have to cut freehand, without a guide), so practice on scrap pieces. Avoid micromanaging the cut; making small corrections leads to a ragged cut. Instead, aim to cut with a smooth, fluid motion. Don't stop and start; keep cutting with constantly moderate pressure.

> **tip**
>
> Even with a good tool and good technique, you may find that a jigsaw cut is less than perfect. That's the time to break out a belt sander or a hand sander with coarse sandpaper, to fine-tune the shape.

A good jigsaw cuts smoothly, with its blade held firmly so it cannot wobble.

Buy a set of jigsaw blades so you will be able to cut tight curves in thin stock and also cut through 2-by lumber.

With most modern jigsaws you can easily change blades without a tool.

Drill

These days, corded ⅜-in. drills are nearly extinct. There's nothing wrong with them; it's just that cordless drills are now powerful enough for most all purposes, and they're easier to use.

THE IMPORTANCE OF PILOT HOLES

If you are driving a screw within 3 in. of a board's end, or if the wood is in any way fragile, driving a screw could cause the wood to crack. Once cracked, there is not much you can do to repair the damage. The way to eliminate these cracks is to drill a pilot hole before driving the screw. This may seem tedious, and you will be tempted to skip the pilot hole. But replacing a cracked board is much more trouble than driving pilot holes.

tip

A pilot hole may be drilled only through the board being attached, or it may be drilled into the receiving board as well. Ideally, the hole in the board being attached should be wider, so there is very little resistance and the screw's head does all the grabbing. But in the real world most people don't want to spend the time to drill two different pilot holes for each screw, so it is common to drill a single hole that is about the thickness of the screw's shaft not including the threads.

In addition to an all-purpose drill (left), consider adding an impact driver (right) to your tool collection. It will easily overcome most any screwdriving difficulties you may encounter.

A magnetic sleeve can hold a variety of screwdriver bits, the most common being Philips and square-drive.

This magnetic sleeve has a reversible bit, making quick work of changing from drill to screwdriver.

Set yourself up with a quick way to drill the pilot and drive the screw. You could change the bit each time—which is actually pretty quick. For even more convenience, buy a sleeve with quickly changeable bits; there are several types available. Or work with two drills, one with a drill bit and one with a screwdriver bit.

BITS AND SLEEVES

Get a complete set of drill bits, and replace bits as they break, dull, or disappear. That way you'll always be ready to drill a pilot hole the right size.

A magnetic sleeve turns any small bit that is inserted into it into a magnet that holds the screw, making it possible to screw with one hand while you hold boards with the other.

DRILLS AND DRIVERS

As long as the drilling and driving is not too difficult, a regular ⅜-in. drill will do the job admirably. Sometimes, however, you may find yourself struggling to drive a long screw through hard lumber. When that happens you could back the screw out and drill another pilot hole. But if you have an impact driver, there will be no problem.

An impact driver acts like a regular drill and turns at a high rate of speed, until it encounters tough sledding. Then it switches to impact mode, where it turns more slowly but with greater torque, so the screw turns with ease.

tip

If you have an old cordless tool set with "NiCad" or "Ni-MH" batteries, you may continue to use them until the batteries die. Then it's time to switch to a tool with Lithium-ion batteries, which hold charges longer and last for years.

tip

Many drills have an adjustable clutch and a "hammer drill" feature. You may never use either of these features, but it doesn't hurt to have them.

POWERING A CORDLESS

A good cordless drill is powered by 18 volts or more. It should have two batteries, so you will always have one that is charged. Cheap chargers keep charging (and stay hot) even after the battery is charged; if you forget to take the battery out, it will shorten the life of the charger or the battery; some cheap cordless tools are notorious for dying after a year or two. Better-quality tools have batteries and chargers with auto shutoff—they hold their charges longer and last for many years.

If you buy a set of cordless tools you will probably get more than one battery. This set has a long-lasting large battery as well as a lighter battery that must be recharged more often.

safety tip

Nail guns have safety features that make it difficult to shoot them like a gun. Still, injuries are not uncommon. Always hold your hand and other body parts well away from the gun, and keep others—especially children—out of the area.

AIR NAILERS

Once a tool owned only by professionals, air nailers are now within reach of many do-it-yourselfers. A typical nailer kit comes with everything you need to get shooting: a compressor, a hose, and three or more nailers. The nail guns each drive nails or staples of a certain size range. For the projects in this book, you may use a finish nailer, a stapler, and a framing nailer.

A nail gun drives fasteners quickly and in one stroke, meaning you can hold the work still with one hand while you fasten. Unlike when hand-pounding nails, the work will not shake while you fasten, which is a great advantage; shaking can cause things to come loose.

A kit like the one shown here is probably not durable enough for professional use but will meet the needs of a homeowner very well. It will probably use strips of nails (called "sticks"), which have to be replaced more often than the coiled nails often used by pros, but that will not be a problem for small projects.

Almost all nails and staples are galvanized, making them suitable for outdoor projects—but not guaranteed against rusting. Plan to hide all the nails, either by filling the holes with wood filler or by covering them with trim pieces.

Tablesaw

If you're lucky enough to have a professional-quality woodworking tablesaw—the kind that hums confidently as it cuts through even thick hardwood without any sign of strain—then you are more than adequately equipped for outdoor projects. If you have budget constraints, however, don't worry: A modestly priced "contractor" tablesaw with a 10-in. blade, the kind most commonly sold in home centers, will be plenty strong and accurate enough for outdoor projects.

FEATURES TO LOOK FOR

In the modest price range you can choose between a tabletop saw, which can be toted around like a heavy suitcase, or a saw with its own stand, which usually has wheels for portability. Here are some signs of quality:

- The table itself should be perfectly flat; check with a straightedge to be sure. Also measure to see that the miter gauge slot—the groove where the miter gauge slides—is perfectly parallel to the sawblade.

- A motor that pulls 15 amps or more will be strong enough to cut through plenty of 2-by lumber.

An inexpensive saw may not allow you to use the blade guard for beveled cuts. If you do work without a guard, be extremely careful.

This fence has a magnifying window that clearly shows how far the fence is from the blade. You'll still want to double-check the measurement with a tape measure though.

- Some saws have blade guards that work only when you are cutting at 90 degrees; a better saw will allow you to leave the guard on no matter what bevel you are cutting at. A better guard will raise up in such a way that it rests flat on the board being cut, rather than being tilted at an angle.

- The miter guide should be solid-feeling, and should have a setscrew for micro-adjusting, so you can be certain that it will be precisely 90 degrees to the blade when making a crosscut.

- A good fence slides easily from side to side (some slide via a crank), and has a distance gauge that accurately tells you how wide the board will be when you cut it.

- It should be easy to raise and lower the blade and to adjust the blade's angle. The adjusting cranks and handles should be large and easy to reach.

- An outfeed support extends outward to support boards as you rip-cut them, and provides enough support for ripcuts of up to 5 ft. or so. (For longer cuts, have a helper hold the board, or construct a support farther away from the saw.) Many saws do not have this.

- Some saws have a fence that can be positioned no farther than 16 in. from the blade. If you want to rip-cut wider than that, get a saw that allows for wider fence positioning.

- Many saws have a dust port to which you can connect a vacuum cleaner. Don't, however, expect to remove all the dust. A moderately priced tablesaw should be used outdoors or with a supplemental dust control system and a dust mask.

tip

Most tablesaws come with an inexpensive blade. By spending $30 or more for a blade with 40 or more teeth, you'll greatly improve your saw's performance.

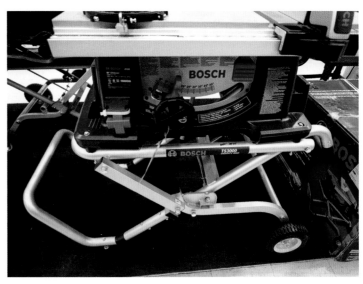

This miter guide slides smoothly in the table's groove without a hint of wobble, and has a setscrew adjuster for achieving precise angles.

This saw has a stand that can be raised and lowered, as well as wheels for easy transport.

USING A TABLESAW

The most common use for a tablesaw is rip-cutting. It also works fine for crosscutting, but it's difficult to crosscut long boards; a power miter saw or a circular saw works better for that.

To make a ripcut, adjust the fence and use a tape measure to check the distance between the fence and the blade. To ensure against kickback, position the fence for an open-throat cut, as shown on p. 34. If the board is long, provide outfeed support so the board will not tilt down as you near the end of the cut. You may need to position a board on a table or sawhorse at the right height so the board can rest on it. Or have a helper hold the board as it

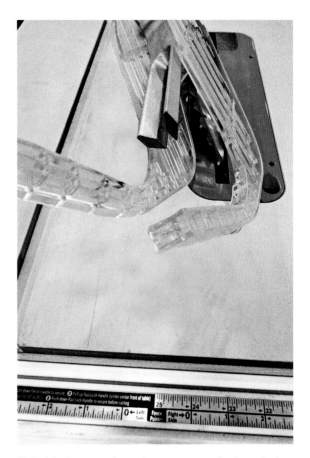

safety tip

Here and elsewhere in the book we show tablesaw cuts with the guard removed for the sake of clarity. When actually doing the work, use the blade guard whenever possible.

This blade guard works no matter the bevel of the cut, and it lies flat on the board being cut, for safer and smoother operation.

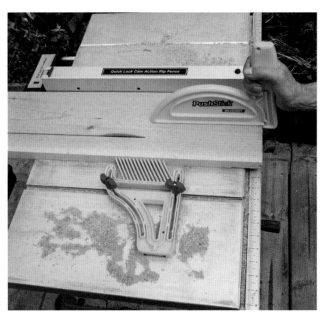

For a safe cut, keep the guard in place and adjust the anti-kickback pawl so it will grab the board and hold it firm if it tries to kick back. When you near the end of the cut, use a push stick to keep your fingers well away from the blade.

If your saw does not have a brace to hold it firm when rip-cutting, you can simply wedge a board to keep it from tipping as you work.

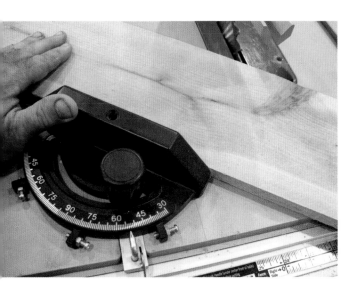

Use the miter guide for straight 90-degree crosscuts, or, as shown here, for mitered cuts.

safety tip

Even if you take precautions against kickback, there's no absolute guarantee that it will not occur. For an additional safety measure, make it a habit to stand to the side of the board you are cutting—out of the possible line of fire should kickback occur.

tip

A helper should grab the front end of a rip-cut board very gently, taking care not to move it to the right or left.

OPEN-THROAT RIPPING

During a ripcut a board may bind between the fence and the blade, leading to dangerous kickback. An anti-kickback pawl is good protection, but it's best to avoid binding altogether. An "open throat" arrangement will greatly help.

Instead of positioning the fence perfectly parallel to the blade, measure and put it at a slight angle, so the place where the board first meets the blade is 1/16 in. closer to the fence than the other end of the blade. When you make the cut, the two sides of the cut will open out slightly, ensuring against binding.

feeds out. Hold the board an inch or so away from the blade, turn the saw on, and press the board's edge against the fence with moderate pressure as you push it through to make the cut.

For a crosscut, make a test cut on a scrap piece first and check that the angle of the cut is correct; make any needed adjustments. Mark for the cut at the front edge of the board. Clasp the board firmly against the guide and push it through to make the cut.

tip

While making a ripcut, if the board starts to wander away from the fence, don't try to make a mid-cut correction; this could cause the blade to bind. Instead, pull the board back to a place where it rests firmly against the fence and cut again.

RIPPING A BOARD IN HALF

If you want to rip-cut a board precisely in half, test the position this way: Measure and position the fence where you think it should be. Just barely start a ripcut, with the board pressed against the fence. Pull the board out, flip it over, and start rip-cutting again. The second cut should line up exactly with the first cut. If not, move the fence a tiny bit in or out.

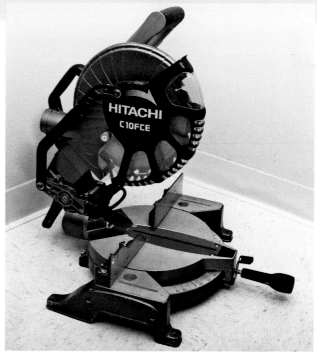

A modestly priced 10-in. chopsaw makes clean, accurate cuts in 2×6 and smaller boards.

Power Miter Saw

Also called a chopsaw, a power miter saw quickly makes crisp, precise cuts. A standard 10-in. chopsaw can cut boards as wide as a 2×6, though if you are cutting at a 45-degree angle you will need to lift the board up a bit to finish the cut. If you want to cut wider boards, consider paying more for a sliding miter saw; it may cut boards as wide as 16 in.

If you are cutting short boards only, you can simply place the saw on sawhorses, a table, or the ground or floor. If the board is longer than 3 ft., you probably need to provide support at the same height as the saw's base—at least on one side, and perhaps on both sides.

Test the saw on scrap pieces before cutting the real thing. Make a cut, then check whether the angle measures a perfect 90 or 45 degrees. If not, follow the manufacturer's instructions for adjusting the saw; it should take only a few minutes to do so.

If cutting results in tearout or less-than-clean cuts, it's probably time to replace the blade with one that has at least 40 carbide teeth.

To cut a series of boards at the same length, drive screws to fasten the chopsaw to the work table. Attach boards to reach the height of the saw's base (two 2-bys will often do the trick). Position a cut board against the sawblade and fasten a stop piece against the other end of the board.

To make a cut, position the board firmly against the back fence. Before turning on the saw, lower the blade until it touches the cut line. Move the board to the right or left as needed for perfect accuracy. Raise the saw, clasp the board firmly against the fence, turn on the saw, and lower the blade to make the cut.

tip

A compound miter saw can cut at a bevel at the same time as it cuts at an angle. None of the projects in this book require a compound miter saw, however some projects will be easier with one.

Router

A simple, inexpensive router quickly rounds over board edges and makes grooves. You can add rich detail to projects by using a bit that creates an ogee or other detailed edge. For the projects in this book, there is no need to get a plunge router.

This inexpensive router can handle any job in this book. It is equipped with a roundover (radius) bit, set at a depth to recreate the rounded edge of a decking board.

A sharp roundover (radius) bit adjusted to the right depth creates an edge that closely mimics that of a 5/4 decking board. This edge may or may not need light sanding.

Choose a router with a smoothly operating depth adjustment. Also check that it will be easy to change bits.

For quick work, choose self-guiding router bits, which have wheels that glide along the board's edge, maintaining a consistent cut line. These bits work only on board edges. If you want to use a router to make a groove in the middle of a board, you will need to use a guide—either a rip guide supplied along with the tool, or a tacked-on board against which you press the router as you make the cut.

A simple roundover (radius) bit, which creates a rounded edge, may be the most useful. If you want to create a rabbeted edge or a fancy detail, there are bits for that as well.

Always test on scrap pieces before beginning to rout. Raising or lowering the depth of a bit can dramatically change the cut profile. For instance, if a roundover bit is set to cut deeply, it will produce a rounded edge plus a slight rabbet.

Joinery

Wood projects can be joined simply with screws or nails. Fastener heads that are left visible may be considered part of the rustic charm. But for a bit more effort you can achieve joints with a more craftsmanlike appearance. The following pages show a variety of ways to make joints that are attractive and strong. All the techniques are pretty straightforward, and none call for expensive tools. In many cases they will add no more than an hour or so to the building time as opposed to installing visible screws.

SINKING AND PLUGGING

With this method, screws do the fastening, but they are sunk below the surface of the wood and the resulting hole is filled with a wood plug so the joint looks like it was attached with dowels. You can make the plugs out of similar-looking wood, so they will be barely visible. Or create plugs from wood of a contrasting color to show off your joinery.

These bits are all self-guiding. Two have guide wheels at their bottoms, while the one in the middle has a guide at the top of the cutting portion.

tip

A "countersink" bit produces a shallow concave hole, just deep enough so the screw head will rest at the same level as the surrounding board. A "counterbore" bit actually drills a hole, so the screw head will sink below the board's surface.

1 Buy a pilot/counterbore bit, which will drill a pilot hole and also create a hole about ¼ in. deep for the screw head to sink into. Also buy a plug-cutting bit of the same size, to make plugs that will fit into the counterbore holes. Some but not all home centers carry these bits; you may have to order them online. In our example, we use ⁵⁄₁₆-in. bits.

2 On a scrap piece of wood, drill holes with the plug-cutting bit, then use a chisel to pry out the resulting plugs. (Or, if they stick in the bit, to pry them out.) Don't press too hard while drilling, or you may distort the shape of the plugs.

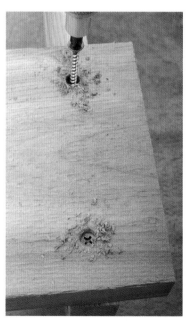

3 The plugs will be visible, so take a little time to position them neatly. Measure from the edges and mark for screw holes that will fall in the middle of the board being attached. In this case, for attaching 1×6s, we measured 1½ in. from each of the side edges.

4 Position the two boards in the way you want them attached. Drill pilot counterbore holes at the marked spots. The pilot bit should drill at least a short distance into the receiving board.

5 Drive screws through the holes to snug the two boards tightly together. The screw heads should sink ¼ in. or so below the surface.

6 Squeeze a single drop of wood glue into each hole. Insert the plugs into each hole with your fingers, then tap gently with a hammer. They will protrude a bit above the wood surface.

7 Wait an hour or more for the glue to harden. Use a small saw (a Japanese pull saw works well) to cut the plugs nearly flush with the board. Don't try to get it perfectly flush, or you may make cut marks in the board.

8 Sand the plugs flush with the board. If the board is smooth, sand with medium pressure. If the board is rough-cut, sand gently so you don't smooth the area around the plug.

THROUGH-DOWEL JOINT

You'll feel like an old-world craftsman if you make joints that use no screws or nails at all, just wood dowels. And it's not hard to do.

tip

Use simple dowel stock, not fluted dowels. Most wood dowels sold at home centers and lumberyards are light-colored hardwood. If you want another color, you can buy from an online source. One such source is McFeely's (www.mcfeelys.com/wood-dowels).

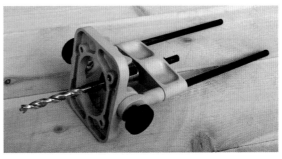

1 If you are confident of your skills, you could simply drill the holes freehand. But if you veer off even ¼ in. the joint will be compromised and the side of the dowel may show. A drill attachment like the one shown, sometimes called a drill-press guide, will ensure that you drill in a straight line. If local stores do not have one, order online. For your dowel rod, buy rod that's about half the thickness of the receiving board.

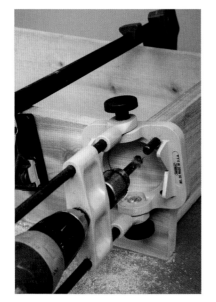

2 Clamp the boards together, so they don't move while you drill. Mark for neatly arranged drill holes, as shown in step 3. Equip your drill with a bit the same size as the dowel you will drive. Attach a drill guide, and drill holes that extend at least 1½ in. into the receiving board.

3 Cut dowels a little longer than the holes you drilled. Squirt a bit of glue onto one and tap it into the hole. Keep tapping until you hit the end of the hole.

4 Use a Japanese pull saw to cut the dowels nearly flush with the board surface. Because the dowels are hardwood, you may need to use a random-orbit sander rather than a hand sander to make them flush and smooth.

tip

Some people prefer the look of dowels that protrude, rather than being cut flush. You may simply tap them in and let well enough alone, or you may use a guide (say, a scrap of ½-in. plywood) to cut them all to the same length.

DADO JOINT

Rather than simply butting one board against the side of another, you can cut a groove, called a dado, into which the first board will fit. This produces a hand-crafted look. The fasteners you use for this joint may be exposed screws, sunk-and-plugged screws, or dowels.

1 Hold the receiving board in place and make sure it is square. Scribe a line on each side of the board to indicate the thickness of the dado.

2 Use a square and a knife to slice lines just to the outsides of the two cut lines. This will ensure against tearout when you make the cuts.

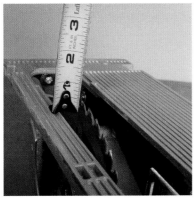

3 Adjust the blade depth on a circular saw to the desired depth of the dado—usually about half the thickness of the board being cut.

4 Using a square for a guide (not shown in the photo), cut the two outside lines, taking care not to go beyond the knife lines.

5 Cut a series of closely spaced lines (called kerfs) on the inside of the dado. Be sure to hold the saw's baseplate flat on the board at all times, so the cuts will be at a uniform depth.

Instead of using a circular saw you can cut the kerfs with a tablesaw. Use a miter guide to hold the board square as you cut. (If you have a set of dado blades, you can set it up and make all the cuts in one or two passes, with no chiseling needed.)

tip

Avoid a common mistake: When measuring and cutting the boards that will fit into the dadoes, be sure to account for the depth of the dadoes, and add that to the boards' lengths.

6 Use a chisel first to pry out the pieces, then to scrape the bottom of the dado. Slip in the board to be attached to make sure it seats well. It should be snug but not so tight that you need to pound on it.

7 Squirt a bit of glue into the dado and tap the board into it. Make sure the joint is flush at the top and bottom. Drill pilot holes and drive screws or dowels.

POCKET-SCREW JOINT

If one side of the joint will not be visible, a pocket-screw joint is a simple and effective joint with no visible fasteners or dowels on the visible side. Buy a pocket screw setup, which includes guides, bits, screws, a clamp, and a long screwdriver bit. Pocket screws can attach boards that are perpendicular to each other, as shown here, or they can attach boards on the same plane, as shown on p. 133.

1 Mark for the locations of the pocket screws. Clamp the guide so it aligns with one of the marks.

tip

These instructions are general. Follow the manufacturer's instructions for positioning the pocket-screw holes, adjusting the length of the bit, and choosing the correct screw, depending on the thickness of the boards being attached (see www.kreg.com).

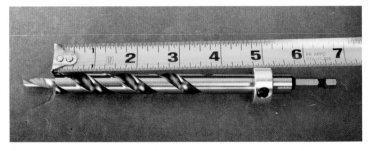

2 Depending on the thickness of the boards being joined, adjust the drill bit's stop so it will drill most, but not all, of the way through the board being attached.

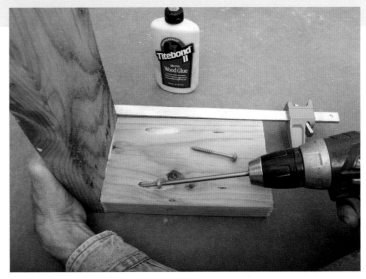

 3 Drill down through the guide until the drill bit's stop hits the guide hole.

4 Clamp the two pieces together in correct alignment. Put the long screwdriver bit on a drill and use it to drive screws of the correct size through the hole and into the receiving board. The screw has a self-tapping tip, so it will not crack the receiving board.

Sanding

Unless you are aiming for a rustic look, chances are you will want to sand your wood project to remove imperfections. This may be the work of only a few minutes, but it is an important step, to give your project a finished look and ensure even coloration when you apply stain.

HAND SANDING

If you are working with hardwood, or if you need to remove more than 1/16 in. of wood surface, you probably need a power sander. But for smoothing surfaces, easing sharp edges, and removing burrs, a hand sanding block is often the best tool because it ensures against oversanding.

Three common sanding blocks: A sponge sander (left), a small carpenter's block (middle), and a drywall block (right).

> **tip**
>
> If your project is made of rough-sawn wood, sanding part of it could result in spots that are noticeably smoother than adjacent surfaces. In that case you may choose to leave the imperfections unsanded.

Sandpapers with a variety of grits enable you to both shape and smooth a number of materials.

Have at least two sizes of sanding block. A small carpenter's block helps you get into most tight spots and makes it easy to shape board ends. A drywall-type sanding block has a larger surface, which makes it easier to evenly smooth out a board's surface. Use a sponge sander for light-duty sanding.

Buy a variety of sandpapers, which usually come in 9-in. by 11-in. sheets. These sheets can be cut (or folded over, then ripped) into segments that fit onto various sizes of sanding block without wastage. Drywall sandpaper strips are made to fit onto drywall sanding blocks, but you can also use half sheets.

The coarser the grit, the more material it will remove—but also the more likely it will be to produce visible scratches. For outdoor projects have on hand 60-, 80-, 100-, and perhaps 120-grit papers. (The higher the number, the finer the grit.) Finer-grit sandpaper is more suitable for indoor projects.

BELT SANDER

This tool can remove a good deal of material quickly, especially if the wood is soft, so use it carefully. In fact, you may think of it as a shaping tool. It's particularly useful for smoothing imperfect curve-cut lines made with a jigsaw. It's also the tool to use for sanding extremely hard wood such as ipé.

Buy sanding belts to fit your tool, ranging from 60- to 120-grit. Always sand with the grain; a single quick sand against the grain can produce lines that are difficult to remove.

A random-orbit sander rotates slowly as it vibrates, for easy sanding.

RANDOM-ORBIT SANDER

A random-orbit sander is midway between hand sanding and a belt sander. It does a good job sanding most materials with little effort, but is not powerful enough to make accidental indentations and will not produce hard-to-remove scratches. Most have pads that attach by a sort of Velcro®, so you simply press them on and pull them off.

Exterior Finishes

In years gone by people sometimes applied a stain, then a varnish or other finish onto exterior wood. But things have simplified in recent decades. While you can choose among a wide variety of stains, oils, varnishes, shellacs, and polyurethanes for indoor wood, exterior projects are almost always coated with a one-step semitransparent stain, a solid-color stain, or paint.

Sanding belts of different grit coarseness can be easily changed on a belt sander.

tip

You may want to apply a perfectly clear finish to maintain the initial look of a board, but that simply won't work. A wood finish must have some pigment to reduce the effect of UV rays from the sun. If you apply only a clear finish, the wood will turn gray.

SEMITRANSPARENT STAIN

Most of these products are referred to as deck or deck-and-fence stains. A semitransparent stain penetrates into the wood fiber and provides a bit of pigment to keep the wood from turning gray. It will highlight rather than hide natural wood tones and grain.

Unlike paint or solid stain, semitransparent stain will not crack, bubble, or peel. To prepare for reapplication, you usually only need to wash or scrape the surface and allow it to dry.

As of this writing, water-based semitransparent stains have improved in durability but have not caught up with oil-based stains, which provide the best protection. Oil-based products may not be available in your area, however. Water-based stains need to be reapplied more often than oil-based products. To learn which products last longest in your area, consult with a paint expert or a local builder.

Most home centers or paint stores will have sample strips that show what the stain will look like when applied to cedar, redwood, treated wood, and so on. These are only general guidelines, of course; your wood may be darker or lighter than the wood used for sample strips.

SOLID STAIN

A solid stain is essentially a thinned paint. (In fact, some people simply add extra water or paint thinner to paint in order to create a solid stain.) The appearance is halfway between semitransparent stain and paint: It allows only some of the wood grain and texture to show through.

These products are usually water based (acrylic or latex); oil- or alkyd-based solid stains perform only slightly better, if at all.

The great advantage of solid stain is that if properly applied it may not need to be reapplied for 5 to 10 years, depending on your climate. You can apply a solid stain over any surface, including one that currently has a semitransparent stain. However, be sure not to apply a water-based stain over an oil- or alkyd-based finish unless you sand it thoroughly; otherwise it will peel and crack.

PAINT

You may resist the idea of painting a project because it hides the natural texture of the wood. But paint has its advantages. There are a nearly infinite number of paint colors to choose from, you can easily change a color by repainting, and paint does the best job protecting wood from the ravages of moisture and sun.

However, paint must be applied completely and any cracks or gaps must be repainted. Otherwise water will infiltrate and the surrounding paint will keep the board from drying out—which can quickly lead to rot and swelling. That's why decks and other large outdoor projects do not do well if painted.

High-quality acrylic and latex paints actually outperform oil-based paints for most projects, because water-based paints have more flexibility.

Water-based paint may have some trouble fully adhering to wood that is not perfectly dry. So the best course is to first apply a coat of oil- or alcohol-based primer (also called white shellac), then apply the paint. Paint that is 100 percent acrylic costs a bit more but will last the longest.

Most types of semitransparent stain and solid stain can be applied in one coat; there is usually no need to cover with a sealer.

A quick coat of primer ensures that paint will stick firmly.

2 planters

CHANCES ARE you already have potted plants that bring cheer to your deck, patio, or yard. But putting those plants into a handsome planter (or three or four) adds a new layer of distinctive beauty to your outdoor room. Choose planter styles and materials to suit the mood you want to set—be it stately, fanciful, or rustic.

A planter can be built to hold soil or to hold a pot. If soil will touch the wood directly, be sure the wood will survive many seasons of wetness. Either use treated lumber rated for in-ground use or apply several coats of sealer to the inside of the planter. Or take your completed planter to a sheet-metal shop and have them fashion a galvanized liner to fit.

The advantage of a pot-holding planter is that you can easily change plants. Grow plants in an inconspicuous spot and rotate the bloomiest ones into the planter. Or purchase inexpensive plants in plastic pots. When you construct your planter, be sure it will hold (and just barely hide) the 5-gal. or 10-gal. pots you plan to use.

PROTECT THE DECK

Pay special attention to drainage. The bottom of the planter should have holes or slots that allow water to pass through freely. Unless the planter will rest on a lawn, provide a substantial drain dish to collect the water so you don't water-stain your patio or deck. Position the planter's drain holes so all the water will drip into the dish.

Tall Fluted Planter

Most planters raise plants only slightly above the ground. If low plants will get lost in the landscape, consider lifting them up with a tall planter. This handsome fellow brings plants up to a more view-able height, and adds a welcome touch of wood. It stands 3 ft. tall and is about 20 in. wide at the top. Its gently widening profile, along with the scallop cuts at top and bottom, gives it an organic feel.

Stained cedar makes an elegant planter for a modest price. The project shown is built with 1×6 (sides) and 2×6 boards (corners). If your planter will be 4 ft. or taller, consider using 5/4 decking for the sides, for improved strength and a more solid appearance. For an airier look, a rougher surface, and a lower cost, use cedar dog-ear fencing for the sides and 5/4 decking for the corners.

MATERIALS

- four 6-ft. 1×6s (or two 12-footers), for the sides
- two 6-ft. 2×6s (or one 12-footer), for the corners
- 8-ft. pressure-treated 1×6 or scrap pieces, for the interior shelves and cleats
- deck screws or stainless-steel screws
- polyurethane construction adhesive, with caulk gun
- stain and finish

TOOLS

- circular saw
- straightedge or chalkline
- tablesaw (optional)
- square
- compass made of cardboard, screw, and pencil
- saber jigsaw
- power or hand sander
- drill with screwdriver bit
- nail gun with trim nails

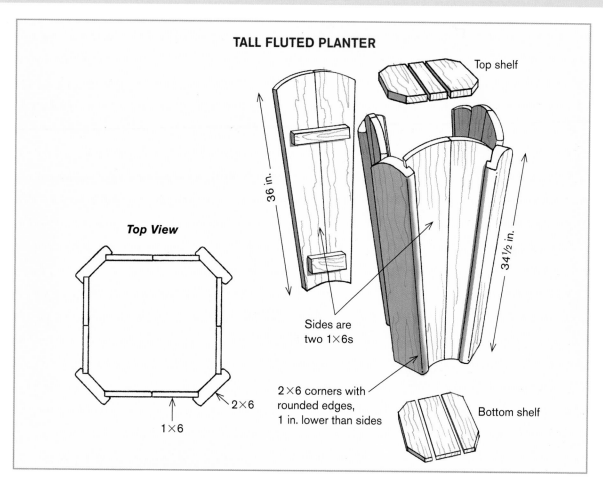

TALL FLUTED PLANTER

Top shelf

36 in.

Top View

34½ in.

Sides are
two 1×6s

2×6

1×6

2×6 corners with
rounded edges,
1 in. lower than sides

Bottom shelf

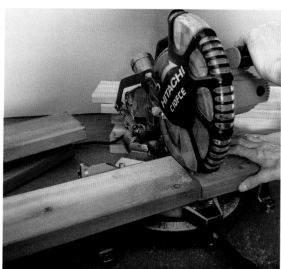

1 From the 1×6s, cut eight pieces 36 in. long.
From the 2×6s, cut four pieces 34½ in. long.
Take care to cut off any ends with splits or other
imperfections.

2 On one of the 1×6 side pieces you just cut,
use a straightedge or chalkline to mark a line
to cut the sloping side. The line starts at the full
width of the board at one end and ends 3 in. wide
at the other end. Use a circular saw to cut the line.

3 Use this cut piece as a template to mark the other boards for cutting. Then cut the other seven pieces.

5 The trickiest part of this project is cutting a 45-degree notch at each side of the corner boards. Steps 6 and 7 have been tested to work for a 2×6 corner piece, but you may find that you have to adjust the dimensions slightly. Practice on a scrap 2×6, and test-fit side pieces to be sure you've got the angles correct. To help orient yourself, mark the end of a 2× scrap as shown, to indicate the direction of the cuts.

4 On a flat surface or pair of steady sawhorses, place two side pieces with their uncut sides butted together, the outward-facing (and better-looking) side facing down. Cut two cleats out of scrap lumber, the width of the two side pieces. Position one cleat with its top edge about 3 in. from the bottom and the other ¾ in. below the desired top of the shelf that will hold the flower pot or soil. Apply construction adhesive to the back of each cleat, and drive screws to attach. Be sure the screws are long enough to penetrate most of the way into the sides, but not so long as to poke through. Repeat with the other side pieces.

6 If you have a tablesaw, adjust the blade to a 45-degree angle. Raise the blade so the very top of a tooth (when turned so it is at the top of its arc) is ⅞ in. above the table. Then adjust the fence so the top of a tooth is 1⅛ in. from the fence.

7 You will cut the notches in two passes. With the blade and fence adjusted to the dimensions shown in step 6, hold the board on edge and pressed against the fence and cut through its length. Then turn the board over and cut the other side, as shown.

safety tip

If your tablesaw has a guard that can remain in place while you are making these cuts, by all means leave the guard in place. If you cannot use the guard (as with this tablesaw), take special care to keep your fingers well away from the spinning blade.

8 Once all four corner pieces have been rip-cut on end as shown in step 7, readjust the saw blade so the top of a tooth is ½ in. above the table. Then move the fence so it is ⅞ in. from the edge of a tooth.

9 With the blade and fence adjusted to the dimensions in step 8, lay the board flat, press it against the fence, and cut through it. This should produce a clean notch; if not, adjust the fence or blade as needed. Turn the board around and cut the other side.

The notch can also be cut with a circular saw. Experiment with scrap pieces until you are sure you've got the right dimensions. Adjust the blade to a 45-degree bevel and to a ⅞-in.-deep cut. Chalk or scribe lines on the board 1⅛ in. from each edge. Use a fence guide to cut the line. Then adjust the blade to cut ½ in. deep and draw lines ⅞ in. from the edges and cut the other side of the notch.

10 To mark the top of the side pieces for a curve cut, make a simple compass (also called a transom) out of a piece of cardboard and a screw, as shown. Partially drive the screw through the cardboard about 8 in. from the top of the boards. Poke the pencil through the cardboard at the other end, and draw the curved line.

11 To mark the bottom of the side pieces for a smaller curve cut, position a paint can 1½ in. from the edge on each side and scribe a line. Mark the tops of the corner pieces also using a paint can; the top of the curve should be in the center of the board's width.

12 Use a jigsaw to cut the curves on the side and corner pieces.

13 If the cut looks less than perfect, use a belt sander or a random-orbit sander to smooth out imperfections and create a pleasing curve.

tip

If you are not skilled at cutting curves, spend a few minutes practicing on scrap pieces before cutting the real thing.

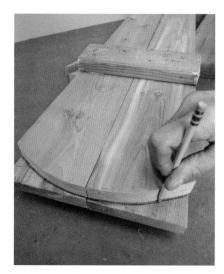

14 Use the first curve-cut boards as templates to mark the others for cutting. Cut and smooth them as well.

15 Have someone help you hold things in place as you assemble the planter. Use a nail gun with trim nails, or drill pilot holes and drive short screws. Check to make sure that the fasteners will not poke through to the outside. Use a square to keep the parts neatly aligned as you work.

16 Measure and cut 1×6 pieces to rest on the bottom cleats to form the bottom shelf. Leave gaps between the pieces, or drill drainage holes. Apply adhesive to the tops of the cleats, drill pilot holes, and drive screws to fasten the bottom shelf pieces to the cleats. Drive small-headed screws through the outside of the corner pieces and into the bottom shelf.

17 Apply polyurethane adhesive with a caulk gun wherever you can reasonably reach a corner. This does not need to be done very neatly, since it will not be visible.

tip

Nailing or screwing while assembling will just barely hold the pieces together; the box won't get firm until you add the shelves.

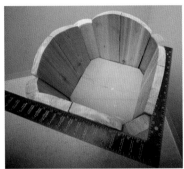

18 Check that the planter is reasonably square and then cut a cardboard template for the top shelf. Cut boards to fit with drainage spaces between, and attach them with screws. Drive small-headed screws through the corner boards and into the shelf.

tip

You may choose to sink and plug the exposed screws on the corners, as shown on p. 38.

19 Sand any rough edges. Apply stain and sealer.

A SIMPLER OPTION

If you want a more geometric look, as well as an easier building project, consider this 3-ft.-tall box with widening sides. Two of the sides are made of three pieces—a straight piece in the middle, and two pieces on each side that are cut as in steps 2 and 3 (pp. 49–50). The other sides are simply made of two straight-cut pieces. Assemble the sides using cleats, and fasten the sides together by drilling pilot holes and driving screws at the corners. Add shelves and drive screws from the outside and into the shelves to firm up the planter.

Short Planter with Legs

This is a pretty simple and straightforward planter, but with some nice details. It angles outward gracefully, and all fastener heads are hidden for a clean look. The supports for the bottom add a simple geometric detail, and the legs, which double as trim that hide the side boards' ends, raise the planter up so it will not sit in puddles of water.

This project was built with cedar dog-eared fencing, a very inexpensive material. Because it is only ⅝ in. thick, pilot holes and screws must be carefully positioned. You may choose to use thicker lumber. The planter may be filled with soil, or it can house a plastic flower pot.

MATERIALS

- ☐ two 6-ft. dog-eared cedar fence boards, for the sides and the bottom supports

- ☐ one 8-ft. cedar 2×2 for the legs

- ☐ treated plywood or other rot-resistant boards for the bottom, about 1 ft. square

- ☐ 1⅝-in. stainless-steel screws

- ☐ exterior wood glue or polyurethane adhesive, with caulk gun

- ☐ primer and paint, or stain and finish

TOOLS

- ☐ circular saw or chopsaw

- ☐ tablesaw

- ☐ square

- ☐ power or hand sander

- ☐ drill with pilot/counterbore and screwdriver bits

SHORT PLANTER WITH LEGS

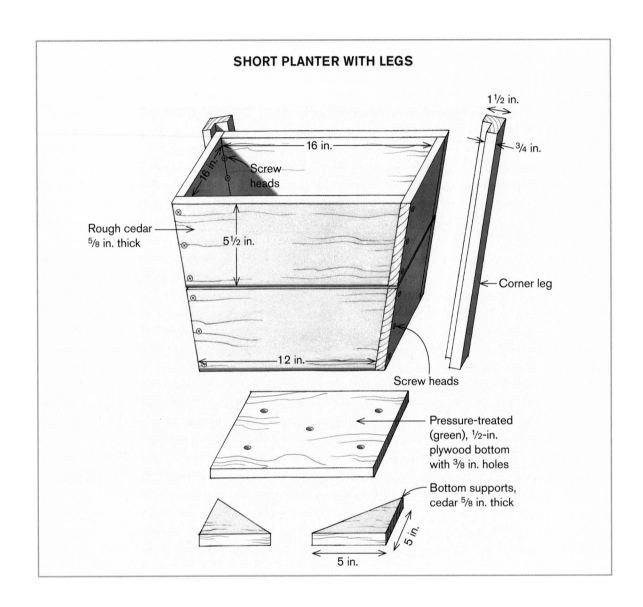

1 1/2 in.

3/4 in.

16 in.

16 in.

Screw heads

Rough cedar 5/8 in. thick

5 1/2 in.

12 in.

Corner leg

Screw heads

Pressure-treated (green), 1/2-in. plywood bottom with 3/8 in. holes

Bottom supports, cedar 5/8 in. thick

5 in.

5 in.

tip

If you build this project out of 5/4 decking or 2×6s, you'll need to use thicker boards for the legs in order to cover the side board ends: A 4×4 will work but might seem a bit massive, so you may want to take the time to rip-cut a 4×4 to a 3×3—which is to say, 2 3/4 by 2 3/4 in.

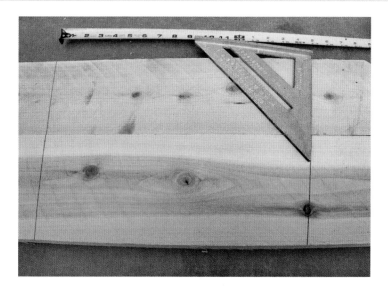

1 Lay a pair of fence boards butted side by side on a flat surface, and mark them to be cut to the dimensions of a side. In our project the top of the planter is 16 in. wide and the sides slope at a 10-degree angle. Use an angle square to mark the angle; it does not need to be precise, but it should be exactly the same on each side.

2 Cut both sides of each piece using a circular saw or a chopsaw. After cutting, lay them side by side. Check that the ends line up precisely, and that the two angle-cut boards line up to form a single straight line on both sides.

tip

Though this is a simple project, it's important to cut all the side pieces with precision. If some boards are off by even ⅛ in., the box will not assemble neatly and the results will look unprofessional.

3 Use the first boards as templates to mark the other boards. Line the first boards up exactly and hold them firmly as you draw the cut lines. Cut the other six boards, checking as you go that they are all the same size.

tip

When cutting a board that has been marked using a template, the pencil mark is a bit larger than the template, and you usually need to cut through the entire thickness of the line—unless your pencil slipped under the template board while you were marking.

4 Because you will be screwing into a thin board, take the time to mark exactly for the pilot holes. On one end of each board, draw three marks at the middle of the receiving board's thickness—in this case, 5/16 in. (or "one-quarter plus"), which is half of 5/8 in.

5 Drill pilot holes at each of the marked locations. Take care to hold the drill straight up and down, at a right angle to the board. If you are uncertain of your skills, use a drill guide (see p. 39).

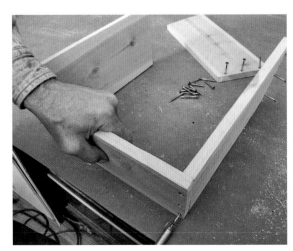

6 Assemble and attach the box in two tiers. At each joint, hold the pieces together precisely, using your fingers to feel that the ends are lined up. Drive stainless-steel screws (1 5/8-in. screws work well) through each pilot hole and into the adjoining board.

tip

Remember that the boards are assembled in a sort of weaving pattern: Each board covers the end grain of an adjoining board at one end and has its own end grain covered at the other end. This arrangement ensures that the box will be the same width at all four corners.

tip

If a receiving board wanders while you are driving a screw, back the screw out, drill another pilot hole, and try again. If this is a recurring problem, you may want to hold the boards in position and re-drill the pilot holes, this time deep enough that they enter the receiving boards.

7 Turn the bottom tier of the planter upside down. Cut triangles from fence boards, about 5 in. long on each side, to use as supports for the planter's bottom. Position them about 1/8 in. back from the front, drill pilot holes, squirt on a bit of wood glue, and drive the screws to attach the supports.

At this point you could stop, and have a good-looking legless planter with exposed screw heads.

8 Cut a piece of treated plywood (shown), pressure-treated wood, or cedar boards to fit in the bottom. If you use boards, leave spaces between them for drainage. If you use plywood, drill five 3/8-in. holes.

9 Out of a 2×2, cut a groove that is 3/4 in. on both sides. To do so set a tablesaw at a blade height of 3/4 in. and position the fence 3/4 in. away from the outside edge of the blade's teeth. Cut one side, taking care to keep the board pressed against the fence. Turn the board around and cut the other side. You can also cut a groove using a circular saw: Use a rip guide (see p. 26), or use a finger guide, as shown.

tip

At the top of the legs the groove will be visible, so it needs to be a neat-looking cut. Whether cutting with a tablesaw or a circular saw, you may need to adjust the blade or the width of the cut so that neither cut line extends beyond the other.

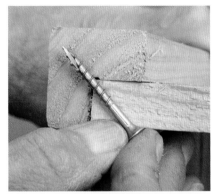

10 Cut the 2×2 into four equal lengths, each 2½ in. longer than the height of the planter at the corners. Use a scrap of 2-by to ensure that each leg is exactly 1½ in. below the bottom of the planter.

11 To avoid exposed screw heads, drive screws from the inside of the planter. Choose screws that will penetrate through most of the 2×2 without poking through. Drive four screws to attach each leg.

12 Use a hand sander to ease any sharp edges, and apply the stain and sealer or paint of your choice.

Stacked 2×2 Planter

This planter has a playful stacked look. (You may find it reminiscent of hats worn by the band Devo in the 1970s.) Building it is a bit like factory work, but of a pleasant kind. Most of the building is done upside down. You'll likely enjoy creating neat stacks of boards that regularly decrease in size, then stacking them in a geometric fashion.

This project was built with pressure-treated 2×2s, which should survive well, especially if they are rated for "ground contact." Cedar and redwood would also work well. If you build with ipé, you can create a more polished-looking creation.

MATERIALS

- three 8-ft. pressure-treated 2×2s, for the sides

- one 8-ft. pressure-treated 2×3, or one 4-ft. pressure-treated 2×6, for the top cap

- treated plywood, 1-bys, or 5/4 decking, for the bottom and feet

- deck screws or stainless-steel screws

- primer and paint, or stain and finish

TOOLS

- chopsaw or circular saw

- square

- router with radius bit

- power or hand sander

- drill with screwdriver bit

- long clamps

- tablesaw (optional)

STACKED 2×2 PLANTER

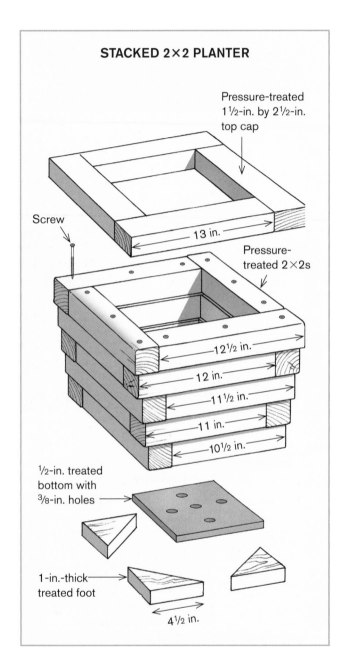

Pressure-treated 1½-in. by 2½-in. top cap

Screw

13 in.

Pressure-treated 2×2s

12½ in.

12 in.

11½ in.

11 in.

10½ in.

½-in. treated bottom with ⅜-in. holes

1-in.-thick treated foot

4½ in.

1 Gang-cut 2×2s in five groups of four, with each succeeding group ½ in. shorter than the previous group: Anchor a chopsaw to a work table. Next to it attach stacked boards that reach the same height as the saw's table. Measure over 12½ in. from the blades and screw on a board to act as a stop. Cut four 2×2s to 12½ in. Unscrew and move the stop over ½ in. and cut four more pieces; repeat until you have five neat piles of 2×2s.

2 Each board will have one end that is visible when the planter is finished. Use a sanding block to remove any burrs or other imperfections on these board ends.

tip
Unless it is kiln-dried with a low moisture content, treated lumber like this needs to dry for at least a few days before staining or painting.

tip

It's easy to get confused, so remember to arrange the boards so that each has one end—and only one—covered by an adjoining board.

3 Working on a flat surface, arrange the four longest boards in a square. Use long clamps to hold the pieces together as you work. (These clamps will actually clasp only half the joints, but that should be enough to enable you to work accurately.)

4 Make a pair of ¼-in.-thick guides: Cut a strip of ¼-in. plywood 1½ in. wide, or rip-cut a ½-in.-thick strip from a piece of 2-by lumber. Position the next group of four boards (½ in. shorter than the bottom boards) in a weaving pattern, so the exposed ends alternate sides from one tier to the next. Use the guide strips to position the second row ¼ in. in from the bottom row. Drill pilot holes, and drive screws to attach. As shown in the photos, drive one screw near each board's end where its end grain is exposed, to tie the tiers together firmly.

5 Continue building upward (and inward), driving three screws through each board.

tip

If you will be using boards instead of plywood for the bottom, you may need to make the legs larger so they can fully support all the bottom boards.

6 Cut four triangular legs, which also act to support the planter's bottom. They should be about 4½ in. long on each side; the exact size does not matter, but they all should be the same size. Use the first leg as a template to mark for the others.

7 Position the legs so they are ¼ in. in from the outside edges of the bottom tier of 2×2s, drill pilot holes, and then drive screws to attach.

8 Turn the planter right-side up. Cut a piece of treated plywood to fit on the bottom. There is no need to attach it. Drill a series of ⅜-in. drainage holes.

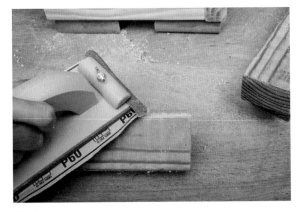

9 If you cannot find 2×3s for the top cap, rip-cut a 2×6 in half and sand the cut edge so it looks like the factory-rounded edge. Out of the 2×3 cut four pieces ½ in. longer than the top 2×2s.

10 Arrange the top 2×3s so they overhang evenly on all four sides. Drill pilot holes and then drive deck screws to attach.

11 Apply exterior wood filler to the screw holes, allowing it to mound up slightly. (If you apply it flush, it may sink below the wood surface as it shrinks when it dries.) Allow it to dry, then sand smooth.

12 Don't paint treated lumber that is moist: The paint will likely peel. If the wood is dry enough so that water sprinkled on it soaks in within a few seconds, it is ready to paint. If sprinkled water beads up, put it in a dry spot and wait a week or more until it dries out; then you can safely paint. Apply a primer, then paint; or apply a stain and sealer. On a project like this spray painting is a good option; you'll probably need two cans each of primer and paint.

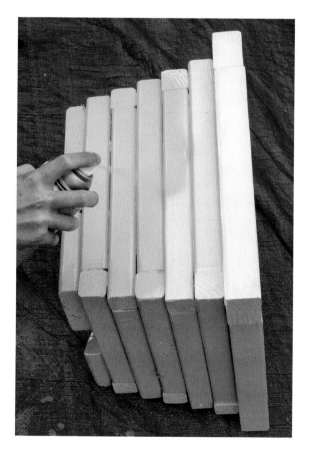

Octagonal Planter

This planter has a classic eight-sided shape and is made of four tiers in an overlapping pattern for a nicely complex appearance. Though the individual pieces are short, it all adds up to a sizable 20-in.-wide planter, enough space for several types of flowers and other plants or a modest herb garden.

The wood is 5/4 cedar decking. It could be built with two tiers of full 5½-in.-wide boards, but ripping the decking in half and building with pieces that are 2¾ in. wide makes for a more interesting checker-board-like design.

For the sides there are only two sizes of boards to cut, all at a 45-degree bevel. Cutting with a chopsaw definitely makes the job go easier, but with a bit of skill you can use a circular saw; it will add no more than a half hour to the time it takes to build the planter.

MATERIALS

- three 8-ft. 5/4×6 decking boards, for the sides and the inside cleats

- treated plywood, or an 8-ft. decking board, for the bottom

- 8-ft. pressure-treated 2×6 or scrap pieces, for the interior shelves and cleats

- self-piloting deck screws

- polyurethane construction adhesive, with caulk gun

- primer and paint, or stain and finish

TOOLS

- tablesaw (optional)

- chopsaw or circular saw

- clamps

- framing square

- router with radius bit

- power or hand sander

- drill with screwdriver bit

- power nailer with nails (optional)

tip

To ensure that you are rip-cutting a board precisely in half, see the technique shown on p. 35.

1 Rip-cut the three decking boards exactly in half; it's important that they all be exactly the same width. A tablesaw is the best tool, but you can also use a circular saw with a rip guide.

2 Equip a router with a radius bit (also called a roundover bit). Set the bit's depth so it produces an edge that is indistinguishable from the factory-rounded edge. Experiment on scrap pieces until you get it right. Run the router along all the cut edges. You may or may not need to use a hand sander to finish rounding the routered edge.

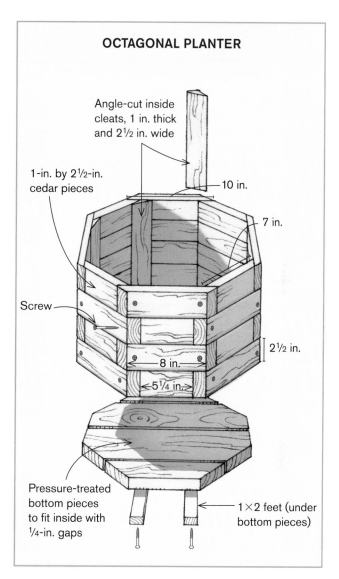

OCTAGONAL PLANTER

Angle-cut inside cleats, 1 in. thick and 2½ in. wide

1-in. by 2½-in. cedar pieces

10 in.

7 in.

Screw

2½ in.

8 in.

5¼ in.

Pressure-treated bottom pieces to fit inside with ¼-in. gaps

1×2 feet (under bottom pieces)

tip

If you do not have a router, you can sand the edges instead. This will take time and patience, and the resulting edge will not be as even as a routed edge, but it will be even enough for an outdoor project.

3 Screw a chopsaw to a table and set it to cut at 45 degrees. Clamp a guide 7 in. away from the blade. Experiment with cutting pieces and adjust the guide's position as needed to produce a piece that is 7 in. long at its long side. Once you've got the clamp right, cut 16 of these short pieces.

4 Set up another stop guide (this one will probably need to be attached to the work table) to cut pieces at 10 in. on their long side. Cut 16 of these long pieces.

5 You'll be driving self-piloting screws, but since they will go in at a 45-degree angle you'll need to drill very shallow holes, just to get them started. Make a simple jig out of a piece of cardboard with a hole in it, to quickly drill holes that are centered on the board's width and 1½ in. away from the cut edge. Drill shallow starter holes on both sides of all the *long* pieces only—not the short pieces.

6 Make a jig to tightly hold the boards while you screw them together: Cut one short piece of wood at 45 degrees on one corner, and screw it onto a work table (or a sheet of plywood on top of sawhorses), and place two boards in position against it. Attach two more small wood pieces as shown, so they snug the boards together in the correct alignment.

tip

If you try to drive the angled screws without a starter hole, they will probably skip out of position and mar the wood.

7 Sand the cut edges to remove any burrs. Take special care with the long pieces, whose edges will be visible.

tip

In this design, the long pieces always overlap the short pieces; both ends of the long pieces are exposed, while both ends of the short pieces are covered.

8 Apply adhesive to one end of a short piece. Set it and a long piece in the jig so the long piece covers the glued end of the short piece. Drive a single screw at each joint. Repeat this for all eight pieces, to make an octagonal tier.

9 Lay a sheet of treated plywood or four decking boards, with 1/4-in. gaps between them, on a table. Set an octagonal tier on top and use a framing square to see that two sides are square. Scribe a pencil line for cutting the bottom piece or pieces, and cut with a circular saw.

10 Lay the cut bottom pieces on the table and use an octagonal tier to check for a fairly snug fit. Cut two small cleats so they overlap the bottom pieces by 7/8 in. on both sides and drive screws to attach. Set the bottom on top (actually, this is the bottom) of the octagon, and drive screws to attach. The cleats will also act as feet for the planter.

11 Set a tablesaw to cut at a height of 2¾ in. and at a 22½° bevel. Position the rip fence ½ in. from the top of the blade. Practice on scrap pieces before cutting the real thing, then rip-cut both sides of a half-width decking board.

12 Stack the four octagonal tiers on top of each other, with the exposed edges in an alternating pattern. Cut eight corner supports from the piece you cut in step 11 to the height of the inside planter, minus a half inch or so. Apply adhesive to each corner support, and attach it to a corner using power-driven nails or short screws. Make sure the fasteners will not poke through.

tip

End grain will soak up stain and sealer like a sponge, so reapply several times with the brush, waiting at least a few minutes between soakings.

13 Sand any obvious imperfections, but don't try to smooth the exposed end grains. Apply stain then sealer.

Wall Planter

Also called vertical planters or living walls, wall planters are an unexpected way to add interest to an outdoor space, whether attached to the wall of a house, a fence, or a lattice structure. Chicken wire and landscaping fabric attached to the face of the planter keep the soil in place but will be nearly invisible once the plants grow. The example shown is planted with succulents, an easy type of plant to keep alive because it can stand periods of drought. If you are confident you will reliably keep your planter watered, you may choose to plant herbs, coleus, or short decorative grasses.

Many designs require you to take the planter down off the wall in order to water it. We've added a baffle on top so you can water the planter in place. Depending on your climate and how often you water, the planter will get wet often, which is why many manufactured wall planters are made of plastic. Here, the horizontal pieces are made of concrete backer board, which will not rot.

MATERIALS

- two 8-ft. 1×4s, for sides, face frame, and baffle
- ½-in. fiber concrete backer board
- ½-in. pressure-treated plywood, the size of the wall planter or about 16 in. by 28 in.
- chicken wire (or "poultry netting")
- landscape fabric
- stainless-steel or deck screws
- polyurethane construction adhesive, with caulk gun
- 3-in. metal straps with screw holes
- primer and paint, or stain and finish
- potting soil (choose one appropriate to your plants)
- peat moss
- small plants

TOOLS

- circular saw, chopsaw, or miter box
- backer board scoring knife, or grinder with masonry blade
- drill with screwdriver and ⅜-in. bits
- hammer
- clamps
- utility knife
- hand sander with 60-grit and 80- or 100-grit sandpaper
- straightedge
- stapler with ⅜-in. staples
- tin snips
- surform tool

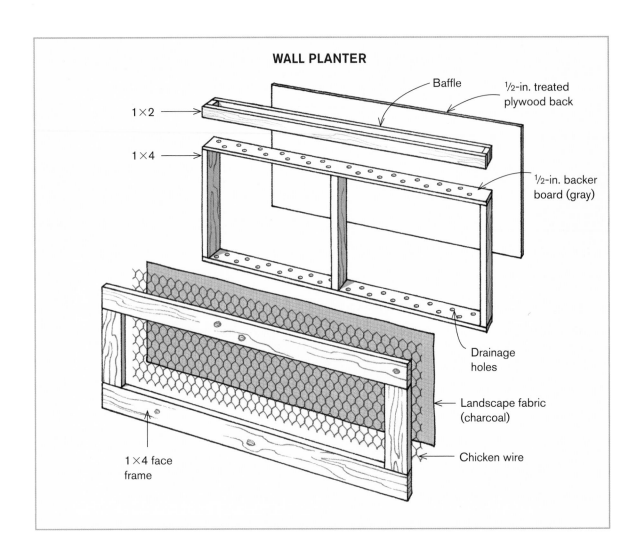

WALL PLANTER

Baffle

½-in. treated plywood back

1×2

1×4

½-in. backer board (gray)

Drainage holes

Landscape fabric (charcoal)

Chicken wire

1×4 face frame

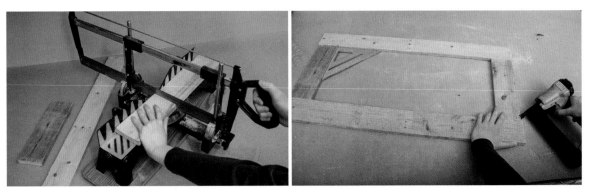

1 Cut the pieces for the face frame. Here we are using pallet wood, for a rustic look. You could use 1×4 or 2×4 ipé or cedar, and use pocket screws (see pp. 42–43) for a more refined look. The frame will attach firmly to the planter box (step 9); for now, angle-drive nails or screws to hold it together.

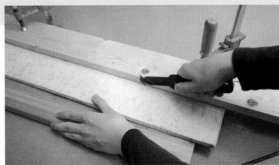

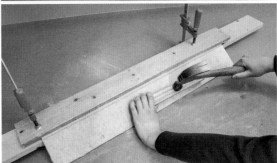

2 With the face frame assembled, measure for the size of the planter box. Keep in mind that you will attach a 2-in.-tall baffle at the top. Size the box so the face frame overlaps it by 1½ in. all around, so the face frame is pretty much the only thing people see.

3 Cut the sides and the piece that runs down the middle out of 1×4. To cut backer board to the same width as the boards, clamp a straight board onto the backer board and score repeatedly using a backer-board cutting tool. Then tap with a hammer and scrap piece of wood to snap the cut.

tip There are two types of backer board. For this project, use the type with embedded fibers (sometimes called "Hardie" board), rather than the type made of concrete and mesh tape.

safety tip Cutting backer board with a grinder or circular saw will produce clouds of dust that are not good for your lungs. Work outside or in a well-ventilated place, and wear a dust mask.

Another way to cut backer board is to use a grinder or a circular saw equipped with a masonry blade (either a diamond blade or a black fibrous blade). Clamp a straightedge to the backer board, against the cut line, and hold the blade against it as you cut. It may take several passes to complete the cut.

4 The cut edge will be somewhat ragged. Use a surform tool or a hand sander with 60-grit sandpaper to smooth it.

5 Assemble the box by drilling pilot holes, then driving screws to attach the backer-board horizontals to the wood verticals.

6 Use tin snips to cut chicken wire to a size that is slightly larger than the box, but smaller than the face frame. Staple the chicken wire to the back of the face frame: Drive a staple in a corner, then pull the wire taut as you drive more staples.

7 Cut the landscape fabric with a utility knife and straightedge, and then staple it over the chicken wire. Keep it taut as you staple and drive plenty of staples to fasten the chicken wire as well as the fabric.

8 Rip-cut a 1×4 board to about 2 in. wide and cut it to the length of the planter to make a baffle on top of the box. Fasten the baffle together with nails or screws, then attach it to the box by driving nails or screws up through the top backer board.

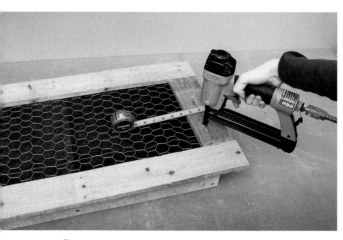

tip

After installing the face frame you may choose to cut back the landscape fabric and chicken wire that is exposed on its back. Use a knife for the fabric and tin snips for the wire.

9 Position the face frame over the box so the overhang is even on all sides. Drive nails or screws to attach the face frame to the wood members of the box. A tape measure helps you locate the boards.

10 For additional strength and to prevent leakage, apply polyurethane construction adhesive to the inside corners of the box, as well as to the inside of the baffle. Allow the adhesive to dry for at least a few hours.

11 Apply the finish of your choice. For a quick and easy "shabby" sort of look, we've mixed two parts paint to one part water and applied with a brush. Use masking tape to protect the landscape fabric.

12 Mix a batch of soil suited to your plants, and add extra peat moss to help it hold together. For our succulents we've mixed three parts cactus potting soil mix with one part peat moss.

13 Turn the planter upside down and pour in the soil mixture. Pat it lightly so it is fairly firm.

14 Cut a piece of plywood to fit over the box and attach it with deck or stainless-steel screws driven into the wood boards. At the corners, attach metal straps for hanging the planter.

15 Drill a series of drainage holes in the top and the bottom of the planter, using a ⅜-in. drill bit. The holes on top will allow you to water the planter while it is on the wall.

16 Plan where you will insert the plants, aiming for even spacing and an attractive distribution of various types. Where you will install a small plant, use a utility knife to cut an X. Poke your finger down into the soil and wiggle it around to make a bit of room for the plant.

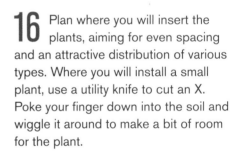

17 When possible, gently pull plants apart and shake away some soil, taking care not to disturb roots. Insert the plant's roots into the hole so it is slightly deeper in the soil than it was in its original pot.

tip

The chicken wire prevents the planting medium from falling out of the planter. So it's fine to cut the chicken wire in a few places, but take care to cut it as little as possible. If your plants cannot be separated to fit in small openings, choose smaller plants.

18 If a plant cannot be separated, you may need to cut a larger opening. Use the utility knife or tin snips to cut the chicken wire as needed, and slice a large X in the fabric.

19 Position your plants to form a fairly even pattern. The spacing should depend on the sizes of the mature plants. Here, small succulents are pretty close together. If you are planting bushy grasses or herbs, wider spacing is called for. Lay the planter down and water it; the water will soak through the landscaping fabric.

20 Leave the planter lying down for a few weeks, so the plants can take root. After they have matured, hang the planter by the straps. When you water the plants, pour water in the baffle and allow it to trickle down through the holes in the bottom.

tip
The first few times you water, dirty water will drip down through the planter. The more you use the planter and the firmer the roots, the less dirty the dripping water will be.

tip
I placed this project prominently, near a sidewalk; nearly everyday someone stops to gawk and offer compliments.

Window Box with Trim

A window box brightens a home from the outside and the inside alike, with flowers that can be seen from each side. This one has a crisp, clean look, with squared edges and a painted finish. The simple trim in front adds classic lines.

Use rot-resistant wood such as the heartwood of cedar or pressure-treated lumber. The cleat that attaches to the wall, as well as to the bottom should be treated lumber. The box can be filled directly with soil, or you can have a local sheet-metal shop make a galvanized insert to fit.

Here, the sill is an architectural feature, so the box is installed just below it. Because the sill protrudes 1 in. from the wall, a 1-in. cleat is used for attaching the box. You may choose instead to attach the box even with the top of the sill.

MATERIALS

- cedar or treated 1×8, for sides, bottom, and trim
- pressure-treated board, for the cleat
- deck or stainless-steel screws
- masonry screws, if attaching to brick
- spray primer and paint

TOOLS

- power miter saw or miter box
- drill with screwdriver and masonry bits
- angle square
- clamp

WINDOW BOX WITH TRIM

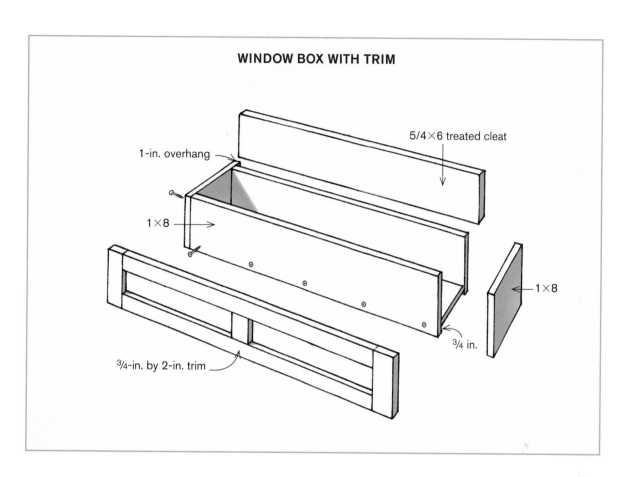

1-in. overhang

5/4×6 treated cleat

1×8

1×8

3/4 in.

3/4-in. by 2-in. trim

1 Measure the sill and determine the desired size of the window box. We've chosen to install a box that extends 1 in. beyond the sill on each side.

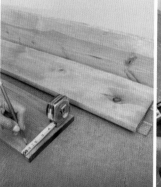

2 Use a power miter saw or a hand miter saw to cut three 1×8s to the width of the planter minus 1½ in. Place the bottom piece on pieces of wood to raise it ¾ in. or so. Mark the sides to indicate the center of the bottom piece's thickness. Drill pilot holes and drive screws to attach the three pieces together.

3 Cut the cleat (which will be used for attaching the box in step 8) to the same length as the three pieces you just assembled. Hold it against the back of the planter and place a piece of 1×8 against the side. Use an angle square to mark the side piece for cutting.

4 Attach the sides by drilling pilot holes and driving screws. These screws will show, so you may choose to sink the screws and fill the holes with wood filler, or countersink and plug (see p. 37).

5 Drill ⅜-in. drainage holes in a grid pattern in the bottom of the box.

tip

When spray painting, always keep the nozzle moving so you don't overspray one spot, which can lead to dripping paint. Spray light coats, allow to dry, then spray more coats.

6 Rip-cut trim pieces 2 in. wide. Hold them in place to mark for cutting. To attach, drill pilot holes and drive screws from the inside of the box and into the trim. Make sure the screws are not so long that they will poke through.

7 Apply primer and paint. You can use spray paint, as shown, or brush it on. Use a product that will last in your climate.

8 If you are attaching to a brick wall, measure to make sure you will drive screws into bricks, which hold better than the mortar. Drill holes through the cleat using a wood screw. Then hold the cleat in position and drill with the masonry bit to mark the location.

9 Remove the cleat and finish drilling the holes in the brick. Use the correct bit for your masonry screws. Replace the cleat and drive the masonry screws to fasten the cleat.

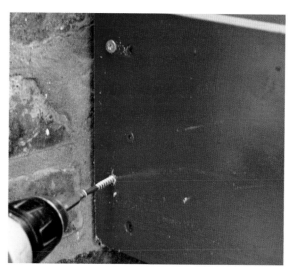

10 Attach the window box by drilling screws through the sides into the cleat from outside the box and through the back into the cleat from inside the box. Add soil and plant.

tip

If the window box is noticeably out of level, insert shims between the box and the cleat to make it come straight out from the wall. You may need to install screws only at the top, then add shims, then drive the other screws.

Window Box with Corbels

This project is a rough-hewn window box with a bit of cabin-like joinery on display. The material is cedar with one rough side, a material that is usually about 7/8 in. thick. For a more substantial result, you could use 2-by lumber instead.

To ensure against mistakes, make the box first, then cut the corbels to fit. The face and back over-lap the sides by 1½ in., in keeping with the style. The corbels in this installation are mostly decorative (though they do add a bit of support), but the box is actually attached at its back. If you need to attach via the corbels, use very long screws to attach the corbels to the wall.

MATERIALS

- 1×8 rough-sawn cedar
- 2×10 cedar, for corbels
- pressure-treated plywood for bottom
- stainless-steel or deck screws
- polyurethane construction adhesive, with caulk gun
- primer and paint, or stain and finish

TOOLS

- circular saw or chopsaw
- angle square
- utility knife
- jigsaw
- belt or hand sander with 60-grit sandpaper
- drill with screwdriver, counterbore, and plug-cutting bits

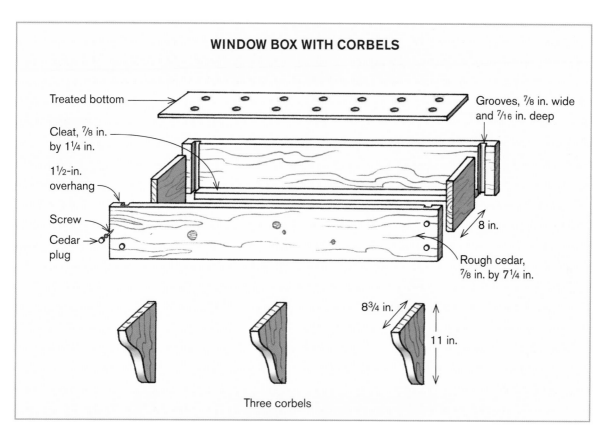

WINDOW BOX WITH CORBELS

Treated bottom

Grooves, ⁷⁄₈ in. wide and ⁷⁄₁₆ in. deep

Cleat, ⁷⁄₈ in. by 1¼ in.

1½-in. overhang

Screw

Cedar plug

8 in.

Rough cedar, ⁷⁄₈ in. by 7¼ in.

8¾ in.

11 in.

Three corbels

1 Cut the cedar for the front and back pieces of the planter to the desired length (the example shown is 46 in. long), and cut the sides to 8 in. long. In the front and back pieces make dado grooves 1½ in. away from the ends on the smooth side (see p. 41 for instructions). Mark the dado grooves using a square and the piece that will fit in the groove; cut the lines with a circular saw set to a depth of half the board's thickness, make a series of cuts inside the lines, and clean out with a chisel.

2 For the front and back pieces, cut a cleat to support the planter's bottom. Rip a piece of 1-by cedar to 1¼ in. wide and cut it to span between the dadoes. Attach with nails or screws to the bottom of the planter.

3 Cut plugs to fill the screw holes (see p. 37 for counterboring and plugging). Drill counterbore holes in the front and back pieces, centered on the dado. Apply polyurethane construction adhesive to the dadoes, insert the sides into the dadoes, and then drive screws to attach. Finish by tapping in the plugs.

4 Once the planter is assembled, cut a piece of treated plywood to fit in the bottom. Drill a series of ³⁄₈-in. holes for drainage and drop it in on top of the cleats.

5 To make a pattern for your corbels, experiment with plates or other round objects. In this example the large plate is used to make the lowest and the topmost curve; a smaller plate makes the middle curve.

tip

The corbels should be the width of the planter minus ¹⁄₄ in., so their fronts are not quite flush with the front of the box, for a neater appearance.

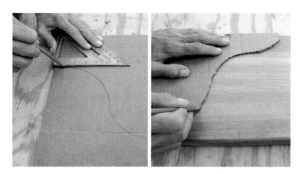

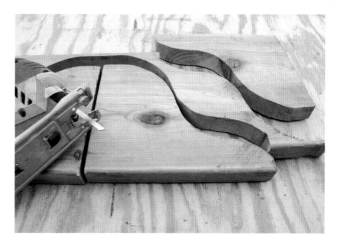

6 Finish drawing the template by using a square to draw straight lines at the ends. Cut with a utility knife, and test to make sure it's the right size by holding it in place. Place the template on a 2×10 and trace the pattern.

7 Cut the corbel pieces using a jigsaw for the curved lines. Practice on scrap pieces if you are not proficient with a jigsaw: Aim for smooth cuts, rather than micromanaging the cuts and making small corrections, which leads to jagged lines.

8 Use a belt sander or a hand sander with 60-grit sandpaper to smooth any uneven cut lines. If the corbel has a smooth side, run the sander across the grain to produce some roughness. You won't match the texture of the rough cedar, but a slightly abraded surface will look more at home.

9 Attach the corbels by drilling pilot holes and then driving screws through the bottom of the planter.

10 Paint or stain and seal the box. (In this example, we applied watered-down paint, for a stained look.) Check for level, then attach the box by driving screws through its back. If that is difficult, use an angle bracket to attach it to the sill.

CHAPTER

3 trellises

A TRELLIS is a structure made with lattice—criss-crossing or intersecting pieces intended to support climbing plants—but a trellis can also be simply decorative. Trellises can add vertical appeal to a yard, patio, or deck.

You can buy ready-made trellises, and some are well made. However, many are flimsy and made of wood that will not last. The connections (and lattice has plenty of connections) are often made simply with a single nail or staple. In many cases you can easily wiggle the joints with your hand. And manufacturers make a limited number of sizes and styles.

Building your own trellis allows you to choose wood that will last, and to join the pieces firmly—perhaps with two nails or staples plus construction adhesive, or perhaps with screws. Also, you can custom-design a trellis to fit a space perfectly or create your own pattern for a personal touch.

Inexpensive trellises can be made quickly using lattice panels, which have slats crisscrossed at 45-degrees. Some of these panels are fairly well put together, while others can easily break or warp. If you build a frame around well-made lattice panels, you can quickly make a trellis that will look good and be fairly durable.

However, for some reason 45-degree lattice just seems cheap, while lattice made with horizontals and verticals feels more elegant. For this reason I typically make my own lattice panels.

Trellises made of metal can look good, but be aware that they can get very hot when the sun beats on them, which can damage climbing plants. Wood is usually cooler.

A trellis may look like a tedious project—all those narrow pieces fastened together! But as the projects in this chapter show, building one need not be a time-consuming project. At times you will be repeating actions over and over, but only for a short while. Many find the process relaxing and satisfying—you may even find it helps clear the mind. And in the end you can create a one-of-a-kind trellis that blows away anything you can buy ready made.

Trellis with Cutouts

This is a basic trellis, with evenly spaced crisscrossing pieces and no difficult joinery. But the addition of some fancy-looking openings add interesting style points. With a power or hand miter saw, making the openings is the work of less than an hour. Here we've simply laid pieces on top of each other and attached with nails and adhesive. For greater strength and a craftsman-like appearance, you could create lap joints, as shown on pp. 98–99.

Your openings could be square or octagonal, but hexagons have a simple elegance all their own. With this project we'll build the latticework, and attach it to a wall. If you want this to be a standalone trellis, attach it to posts, as shown for the Variable-Spaced Trellis with Lap Joints on p. 100.

If you want to paint or stain/seal the lattice, apply several coats. Recoating will be difficult after the plants climb.

MATERIALS

- ☐ cedar, redwood, or treated 1×8

- ☐ nails or screws

- ☐ polyurethane construction adhesive, with caulk gun

- ☐ screws and spacers, or stakes, as needed to attach to wall or ground

TOOLS

- ☐ tablesaw or circular saw with rip guide

- ☐ clamps

- ☐ square

- ☐ power or hand miter saw

- ☐ jigsaw or small hand saw

- ☐ power nailer, or drill with screwdriver bit

1
Rip-cut the lattice pieces. For this project, we took 1×8s, which are 7¼ in. wide, and ripped five pieces that are 1⅜ in. wide from each. (When figuring how many pieces you can get out of a board, include ⅛ in. for the kerf, or the thickness removed by the saw-blade.) If you don't have a tablesaw, cut with a circular saw equipped with a rip guide.

tip

If your trellis will be wider than it is tall, you can mark the horizontals rather than the verticals— there will be fewer of them.

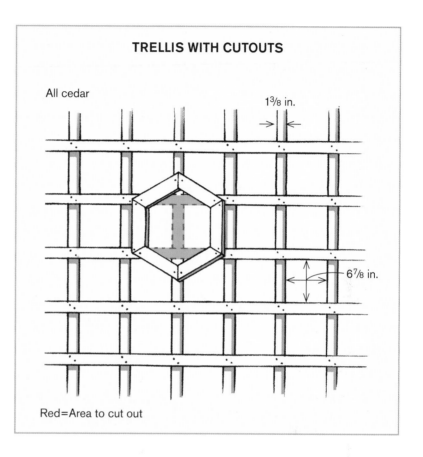

TRELLIS WITH CUTOUTS

All cedar

1⅜ in.

6⅞ in.

Red=Area to cut out

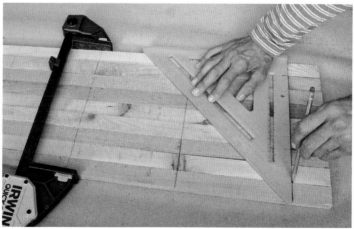

2
Lay the pieces that will run vertically together on a flat surface and clamp them so the ends are flush with each other. Mark for even spacing of the horizontals. Use a framing square or a large angle square (as shown) to draw light lines. In this example we've spaced the lines 8 in. apart, which will produce openings 6⅞ in. wide.

3 Cut a spacer guide out of scrap wood. Lay the slats on a large flat surface, spaced evenly apart. Using your layout lines as a guide, squirt small dabs of construction adhesive where the joints will be. Put the spacer between two verticals to establish the correct spacing and place a horizontal on top of the verticals (or vice versa). Drive two short nails or staples into each joint.

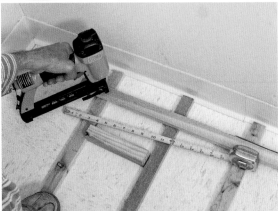

tip

Our spacer is 6⅞ in. long, to produce square openings. You may choose to use a spacer that is shorter or longer, for rectangular openings.

4 Continue aligning the pieces using the spacer and the layout lines. Install the top and bottom pieces first. Take care to always stay on the same side of the layout line. If possible, press boards against a straight wall or two to keep things straight and square.

5 Continue joining the horizontals to the verticals, gluing and fastening each joint, until you have completed the basic trellis. Remember to hold the spacer against the just-nailed slat to ensure that the spacing is even both horizontally and vertically.

tip

If you want smaller or larger openings, have a little fun experimenting with different lengths. Even a difference of an inch in the length of the pieces will result in a significantly larger opening.

6 Cut the pieces for the openings. To make a hexagon, cut the ends of six pieces at 30 degrees. For an opening 11½ in. wide (or 13½ in. from tip to tip), cut each piece 6¾ in. long. Position the saw at the 30-degree mark and clamp a simple stop guide, as shown, to keep all the pieces exactly the same length.

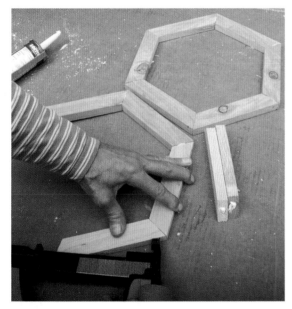

7 To assemble the hexagons, dab adhesive on the end of a cut piece, hold this piece flat against another cut piece, and power-drive a nail (as shown). If you don't have a power nailer, drill pilot holes and drive small-headed screws. (Don't try hand-nailing; the pieces will move around too much while you work.)

8 Nail the hexagon onto the trellis in an attractive position. Usually it looks best to place it symmetrically in relation to the horizontals and verticals. Fasten to the trellis with nails or screws.

9 Use a jigsaw to cut the opening. Carefully align the saw's blade against the inside of the hexagon as you cut; take care not to cut the hexagon itself.

10 Depending on the position of the hexagon, you may need to add small fill-in pieces so you can attach any lattice pieces that are hanging loose. Apply a dab of adhesive, insert the piece, and drive a nail or screw.

11 A trellis like this can be attached to freestanding posts in the ground or, as shown here, can be attached to a fence or wall. Use short sections of copper or plastic pipe as spacers to keep the trellis about 2 in. away from the wall (farther if you will grow thick vines). Drill pilot holes and drive wood or masonry screws, as needed, to attach.

Variable-Spaced Trellis with Lap Joints

This project lets you arrange lattice pieces as you see fit. If you really like our design, you can follow it. Or use the principles shown in this project to create your own design. It's not as complicated as you might expect.

We've opted for a design that is semi-regular in spacing, in both directions. The spacing varies, but with a sort of consistency. The verticals vary in height, with different-length pieces on each side of a central piece in a mirror-image arrangement. The horizontals are all the same length and vary in spacing in a repeating pattern. You may opt for more or less randomness.

This trellis achieves a certain stateliness (perhaps to offset its partial chaos) by lap joinery: The verticals and horizontals meet with dadoes, so they nest inside each other. In keeping with the casual joinery of this book, we've made the dadoes shallow, so the laps are only partial.

You could use design aspects of this project with simpler joinery—just place the pieces on top with no dadoes, as in the Trellis with Cutouts, p. 90. Similarly, you could use the dado joinery and build a trellis with uniform spacing. Anchor the trellis to the ground with posts (step 17), attach it to a wall (facing page), or just lean it against a wall.

MATERIALS

- treated 1×2, eight at 8 ft. and four at 6 ft.

- treated 2×2, two at 8 ft.

- short stainless-steel screws

- polyurethane construction adhesive, with caulk gun

- primer and paint, or stain and finish

TOOLS

- draftsman's ruler (optional)

- drill with screwdriver bit

- clamps

- framing square or a large angle square

- circular saw

- power miter saw (optional)

- router with dado bit, or hammer and chisel

VARIABLE-SPACED TRELLIS WITH LAP JOINTS

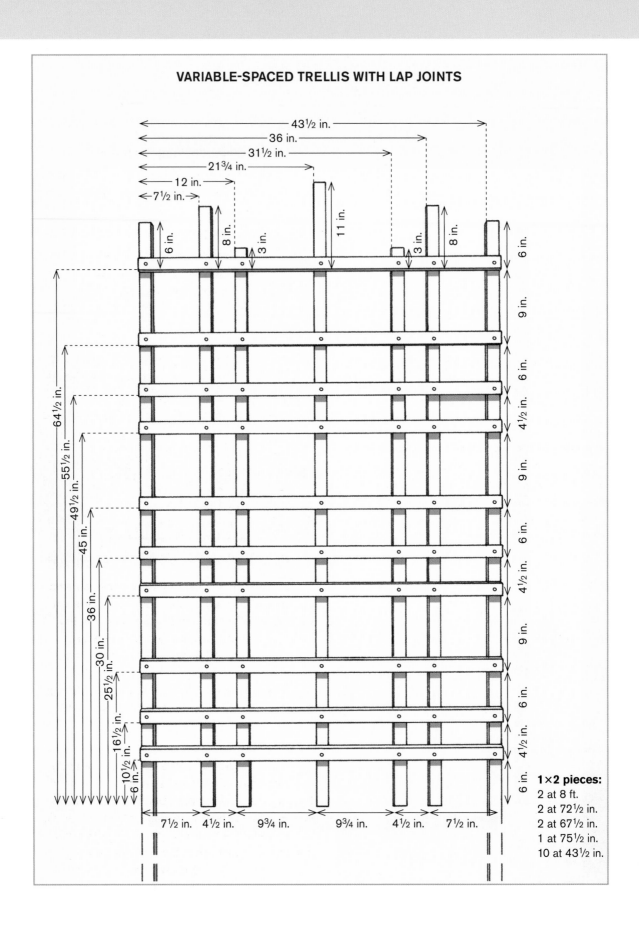

1×2 pieces:
2 at 8 ft.
2 at 72½ in.
2 at 67½ in.
1 at 75½ in.
10 at 43½ in.

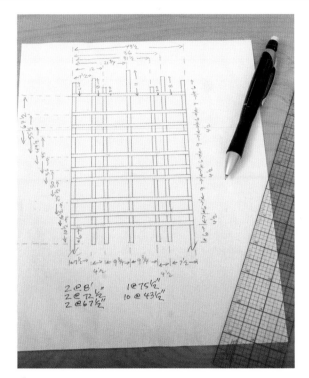

1 Design your trellis by making a scale drawing. A draftsman's ruler, as shown, makes it easy to draw parallel lines. Make the width of the trellis pieces accurate, to gain a clear idea of how it will really look. Give the locations of each piece by indicating one side, rather than the center. Also make a cut list (shown in purple ink on this drawing).

tip

Computer drawing programs, many of which are available for free or for very low prices, will enable you to quickly rearrange the lattice pieces. It may take a few hours or more to learn what you need in order to draw a simple structure like this.

2 Double-check your drawing's measurements before you start cutting the 1×2 boards. (In particular, make sure you take into account the width of the last horizontal and vertical boards.) For this project, all the horizontals are the same length, there are three pairs of same-length verticals, and there is one center vertical. Cut the boards with a circular saw or power miter saw.

3 Prime the pieces, as we have done, or apply a first coat of stain and sealer. (You will need to touch up the finish later, but that will be much easier than doing all the painting after the trellis is built.) Clamp the horizontal pieces together and mark for the locations of the verticals. To keep from getting confused, draw an X on the side of the line where the cross piece will lie.

5 Set a circular saw to cut to a depth of ¼ in. This will result in partial lap joints, rather than the half-lap joints that are often used for fine woodworking. If you will use a router to clean out the middle of the dadoes, equip it with a dado bit and set the bit to the same depth.

4 Use a framing square or a large angle square to mark across the pieces. Then lay a piece of the correct width along the lines and use it as a template to draw a parallel line.

tip

Because 1×2s have rounded edges, it's best to make the dadoes shallow. If you make them half the thickness of the boards, the joints will look odd.

6 Using a large angle square as a guide, cut to the insides of each line with the circular saw. Make sure that the resulting dado will be the correct width for the crossing pieces.

8 Press the router against the guide as you cut the first pass. Then place a rip-cut board against the guide to hold the router in the correct position for cutting on the other side. (Again, experiment on scrap pieces to see how wide the ripped board should be.) Router the two sides, then router out the center of the dadoes.

7 At this point you could make a series of circular saw cuts and clean out the middle with a chisel, as shown on pp. 41–42. But if you have a router, using it will be easier for all these dadoes. Screw a guide board parallel to the line to keep your router from wandering outside the lines. (Experiment on scrap pieces to find how far from the lines the guide should be positioned.)

tip

Experiment cutting dadoes on scrap pieces, to make sure you get the depth of cut right, and also to see that the width is correct so the crossing pieces fit together snugly without being too tight; a $1/16$-in. gap will be easily filled with paint.

9 Clamp the verticals configured as they will end up. (In this case, the bottom edges of all the boards except the outside ones will be at the same level.) Measure and mark for the dadoes as you did for the horizontals.

10 Cut the dadoes as you did for the horizontals. You will need to move the clamp once or twice as you work. Test-fit the crossing pieces to see if you need to slightly widen some of the dadoes.

11 Paint the pieces, or apply stain and sealer. Fill in the dadoes with paint, then finish with light strokes for a smooth appearance. Allow the paint a day or more to dry.

12 Lay the verticals (or horizontals) on a flat surface, dadoes facing up. Here we've laid the five middle verticals but not the two outside pieces, so they can be pressed against a wall for easy alignment. Lay the horizontals (or verticals) on top, with the dadoes aligned.

13 Apply a dab of construction adhesive for each joint. Tap with a hammer and a shim or scrap piece of wood to snug the joints.

OVAL-HEAD SCREWS

For a finished look, we're using oval-head screws, which have a slightly rounded look when installed. Mark the drill bit for the pilot holes so it drives through the top piece but only slightly into the bottom piece, for a firm grip.

14 Drill a pilot hole, then drive a screw into each joint.

16 If any gaps are wider than $1/16$ in., fill them with wood filler. Touch up the joints with paint to achieve a neat appearance.

15 Continue fastening. In our example, the trellis is turned around to attach the two longer outside vertical pieces.

17 If the trellis will stand alone, attach the outside pieces to a 2×2 or larger piece. Dig a post hole at least 2 ft. deep, set the post in, and check for level in both directions as you tamp soil in the hole.

Fan Trellis

This fan trellis is a classic backyard ornament that's quick and easy to build, and fun too. It's a great project to build with a child (apart from the rip-cutting, of course), because it seems to take shape magically as you spread the fan apart. You can anchor it to the ground, attach it to a wall, or simply lean it in place and allow climbing plants to supply all the support you need.

MATERIALS

- one 8-ft.-long piece of 5/4 decking (1 in. thick and 5½ in. wide)

- long deck screws

- primer and paint, or stain and sealer

TOOLS

- tablesaw, or circular saw with rip guide

- drill with screwdriver bit

- clamp

- square

FAN TRELLIS

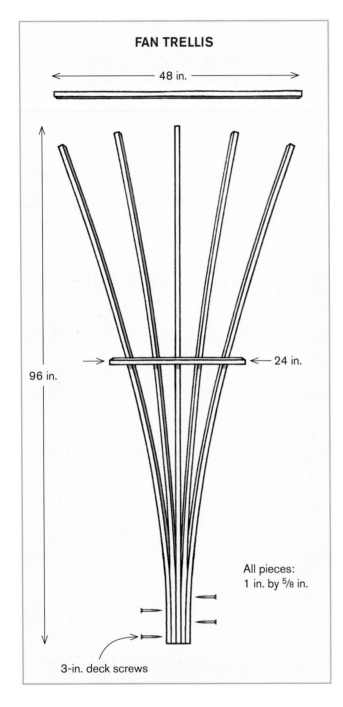

48 in.

96 in.

24 in.

All pieces:
1 in. by 5/8 in.

3-in. deck screws

tip

Choose a decking board that is nearly or completely free of knots. If a ripped piece has a knot, it is likely to crack when you bend it.

1 Rip-cut the 5/4 decking into pieces between ½ in. and 5/8 in. thick. You will need seven pieces. Prime and paint, or apply stain to your pieces.

2 Line up five of your pieces on end against each other, with their bottoms aligned. Drill pilot holes and then drive four screws, two from each side, within 8 in. from the bottom. The screws don't have to reach all of the pieces, but they should reach most of them.

3 Cut one of your leftover two pieces to 48 in. and one to 24 in.; these will run horizontally. Position the 48-in. piece with its center 6 in. down from the top of the middle vertical piece. Drill a pilot hole and drive a screw to fasten.

4 Check that the horizontal and the middle vertical pieces are square to each other. Splay an outside vertical piece until it is 4 in. from the end of the horizontal, and fasten.

5 Splay the other outside vertical piece and fasten it. Then position the middle pieces in the middle of the horizontal and fasten them. Next, attach the 24-in. horizontal so it overhangs the verticals by 2 in. on each side.

4 outdoor furniture

IF BUILDING a planter or a trellis gives you satisfaction and a sense of pride in your accomplishments, then making furniture will at least double those pleasures. The projects in this chapter, if carefully built and maintained with stain or sealer, are genuine candidates for heirloom status. And the act of building them can be a memorable and fun experience.

You may think that professional-looking furniture is out of your reach, but this chapter will show you how to build great-looking furniture with easy joinery. Furniture made for outdoor use can be a bit more rugged than indoor furniture, which means that standard carpentry tools—even a circular saw, and certainly a low-priced tablesaw, for instance—can meet the challenge.

Simple joinery can be just as attractive and strong as joints made with professional-level tools and skills. If you already have the tools and know-how to make a mortise-and-tenon or blind dowel joint, then go ahead. But attaching with screws and plugs is just as effective, and feels right at home in the great outdoors.

You don't have to build with expensive lumber, either. Cedar, or even pressure-treated wood that has been stained, will work fine. Take the time to choose boards carefully, so there are no obvious flaws. And for most projects, a router equipped with a roundover bit will magically transform rough saw-cut edges into professional-looking slats.

Adirondack Chair

Nothing says "chill, but in a classy way" like an Adirondack chair. It is probably the most popular piece of outdoor furniture in the nation. Though sometimes associated with seaside resorts, it is equally at home on a deck, patio, or lawn. Its iconic appearance sets the tone for relaxation.

Why is the Adirondack so well loved? First, comfort: It is probably the most relaxing all-wood chair to sit in. We say "sit in" rather than "sit on" because its angled seat and back cause you to lean back and settle in, so you are half sitting and half reclining. Cheaper and simpler Adirondacks have flat seats and backs, but a true Adirondack must be curved in both places, to better mold to the human body. And the back rises high in the air, so you can rest your head against it if you choose.

Second, there are those large arm rests, perfect for setting drinks, a small snack plate, a magazine, your sunglasses . . . all those things that help make summer relaxing.

And finally, there's the way it looks. It's a complex-looking piece of furniture, a work of art. Hundreds

MATERIALS

- two 8-ft. cedar 1×8s, for seat and back slats and arm rest supports
- two 8-ft. cedar 5/4×6 decking boards, for arm rests, apron and stretcher, back supports, and front legs
- one 8-ft. cedar 2×6, for bottom legs
- 2-in. stainless-steel screws
- wood plugs (plus plugs that you cut yourself)
- polyurethane construction adhesive, with caulk gun
- exterior wood glue
- stain and sealer, or primer and paint

TOOLS

- tablesaw or circular saw
- chopsaw, power miter saw, or hand miter saw
- jigsaw
- drill with screwdriver, pilot/counterbore, and plug-cutting bits
- router with roundover bit
- framing square
- angle square
- compass
- trammel (long compass) made of cardboard, screw, and pencil
- flexible curve marker
- belt sander
- hand sanding block

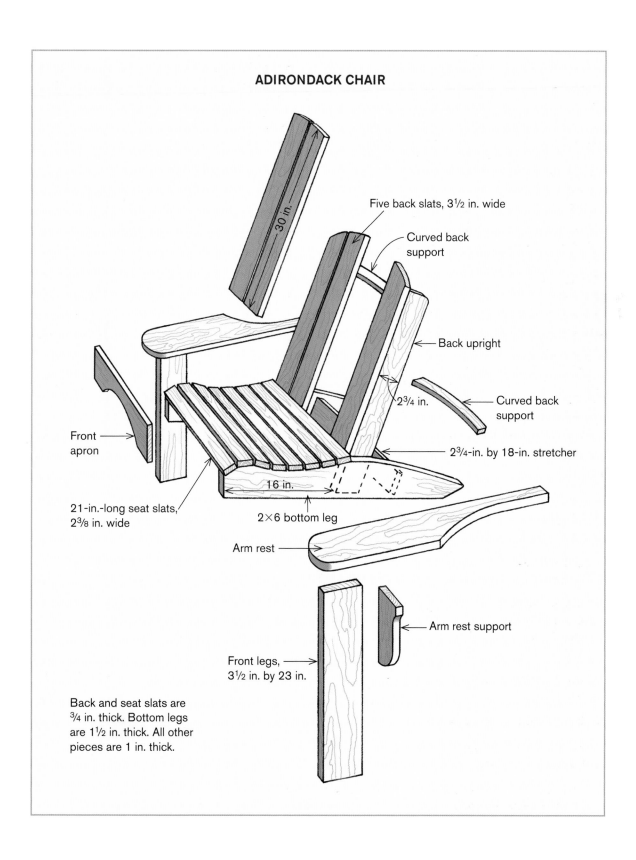

ADIRONDACK CHAIR

30 in.

Five back slats, 3½ in. wide

Curved back support

Back upright

2¾ in.

Curved back support

2¾-in. by 18-in. stretcher

Front apron

16 in.

2×6 bottom leg

Arm rest

21-in.-long seat slats, 2⅜ in. wide

Arm rest support

Front legs, 3½ in. by 23 in.

Back and seat slats are ¾ in. thick. Bottom legs are 1½ in. thick. All other pieces are 1 in. thick.

ADIRONDACK CHAIR PATTERNS

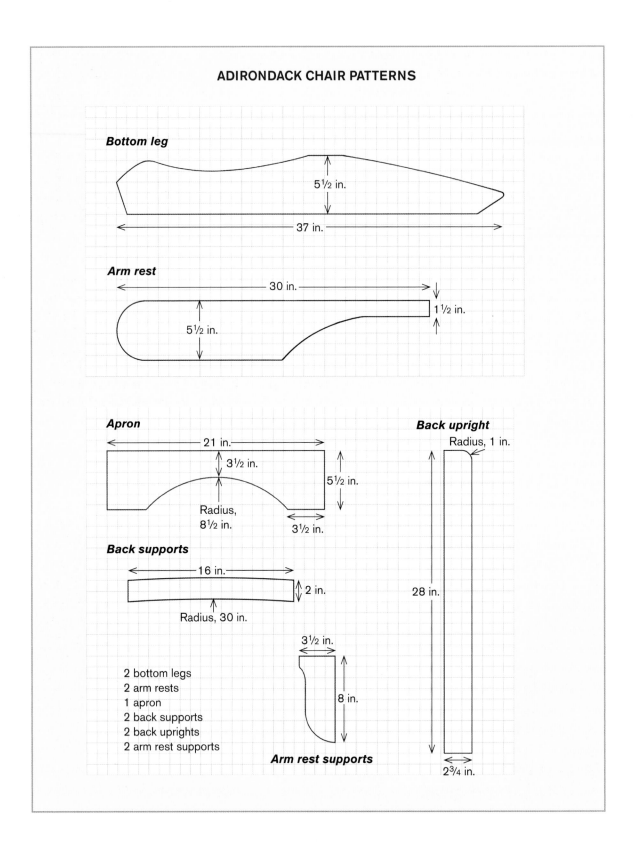

Bottom leg

5½ in.

37 in.

Arm rest

30 in.

1½ in.

5½ in.

Apron

21 in.

3½ in.

5½ in.

Radius,
8½ in.

3½ in.

Back upright

Radius, 1 in.

28 in.

2¾ in.

Back supports

16 in.

2 in.

Radius, 30 in.

2 bottom legs
2 arm rests
1 apron
2 back supports
2 back uprights
2 arm rest supports

3½ in.

8 in.

Arm rest supports

of designs have been generated by architects and furniture makers over the years. And there are countless ways to vary your own design: Seat backs can be cut in any number of patterns, the pieces that support the arm rests can be designed in different ways, and so on.

Expect to take a day or two to build this project, depending on your skill level. A router with a round-over bit is an essential tool.

The project as shown uses cedar, which resists rot and is lightweight. Cedar is easily shaped with a belt sander—which is often needed after cutting a curve with a jigsaw. Redwood and mahogany are other good options. High-quality pressure-treated wood is another good choice, especially if you plan to paint it. If you build with ipé or another heavy hardwood, shaping with a sander will be difficult, and it may take two people to pick the chair up and move it.

Once you've built this chair, you may want to accessorize it with an Adirondack ottoman or table or both, which are the next two projects in this book.

1 Cut the 2×6 to length to make the bottom legs. Cut 5/4 decking to length for the arm rests, the apron, and the curved back supports. NOTE: Cut the back supports (which will later be curve-cut) an extra ¼ in. long; you will cut them precisely when you install them (step 16). Rip-cut 5/4 decking in half (making pieces 2¾ in. wide) for the stretcher and the back uprights. Cut the front legs to 23 in. by 3½ in. Use a chopsaw or hand miter saw to cut the pieces to length. (Refer to the patterns for lengths.)

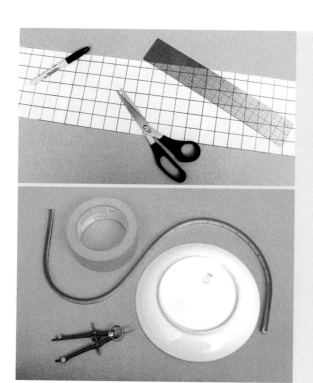

TOOLS FOR CURVES

Projects in this chapter sometimes call for curves, and there are a variety of ways to draw them. If the project gives a graph-paper illustration for a piece, the grid will be in 1-in. squares. To make your own grid to match, start with graph paper (which is usually 4 squares to the inch) and use a marker and draftsman's ruler to make a 1-in. grid. You can then cut the paper to the width of the board (here, 5½ in.).

To mark simple arcing curves that are fairly tight, use a plate or roll of tape (as shown here) or a large plastic bucket. For a more complex curve, use a bendable curve marker, available at office supply stores. For very tight arcs, use a compass.

2 Use a compass to mark one of the back upright supports for a 1-in. radius cut. Use a jigsaw for the cut, then use the piece as a template to mark for the second back upright.

3 To mark an arm rest for the complex curve cut, position a bendable curve marker on 1-in. graph paper (see sidebar on p. 109) and bend it carefully until it matches the desired curve. Place the curve marker on the board and mark for the curve cut.

4 Use a compass to mark the front of an arm rest for a curve cut. Cut both curved lines with a jigsaw. Belt sand (step 5), then use the first arm rest as a template for marking and cutting the second.

 tip

When cutting with a jigsaw it's usually more important to achieve smooth curves than it is to stay precisely on the line. If you start to stray from the line, don't make a sudden turn, instead aim for a wide, sweeping arc.

5 For the arm rests and for all other curve cuts, use a belt sander to gently shape the curve until it is pleasing to look at, with no visible imperfections. Hold the sander's belt straight upright as you sand to avoid creating an unwanted bevel, and exert only moderate pressure. Keep sanding until you are happy with the curve before proceeding to the router, which will only follow lines and not correct them.

6 Good edge routing is essential for a great-looking piece of furniture. Equip a router with a roundover bit and experiment on scrap pieces until it is correctly adjusted and you feel proficient: It should produce an edge that is just like the rounded edge of a piece of 5/4 decking. Hold the router flat on the board as you press against the board's edge and move it along. Rout all cut edges.

7 The routed edge may have some imperfections that need to be cleaned up. A hand sanding block is usually the best tool; a belt sander may take away too much.

8 Use a curve marker and 1-in. grid paper (see step 3) to mark a 2×6 bottom leg for curved cuts. (The curve marker is long enough to mark only one curve at a time.) Cut the front angle with a circular saw and cut the curves with a jigsaw.

9 Belt sand the curves (see step 5), then use the first bottom leg as a template for the second. Sand the edges lightly; there is no need to use the router.

10 To mark a curved back support for cutting, make a large compass out of a piece of cardboard, a screw, and a pencil. Place the board square to the table you are working on. Drive a screw through the cardboard 30 in. away, at the same distance from the table's edge as the center of the curve on the board. Position the curve so as to use the total width of the board. Poke the pencil through the cardboard and draw the curve. Move the compass up 2 in. and draw the other side of the curve.

11 Cut this piece with a jigsaw, sand with a belt sander (step 5), then use it as a template for the other back support. Rout and hand sand the front and back edges, but not the ends (steps 6–7).

12 To mark the front apron for a curve cut at the bottom, use a compass to draw a curved line with a radius of 8½ in. The curve should end 3½ in. from the edge on each side. Cut with a jigsaw, then belt-sand, rout, and hand sand (steps 5–7).

13 Attach the stretcher between the two bottom legs, a few inches from the back ends. Check for square and see that the stretcher is the same distance from the back of each leg. Attach the apron to the front of the bottom legs, its ends flush with the outside faces of the legs. To attach, drill pilot/countersink holes, then drive screws (see p. 38).

14 Measuring along the bottom of a bottom leg, mark the point 16 in. from the front of the leg (not including the thickness of the apron). Starting at this point, use an angle square to mark a line on the inside of each leg that is 10 degrees less than square, as shown. This will be the angle at which the seat back reclines in relation to the seat.

15 Attach the back upright supports to the inside of each leg, following the line you drew in step 14. Drill pilot holes and drive several widely spaced screws into each joint.

17 Attach the front legs so they raise the top of the apron 16 in. above the ground. The front of the front legs should be flush with the face of the apron.

16 Test-fit the curved back supports, which fit between the upright supports. They should be snug, but not so tight as to cause the upright supports to splay out. Cut as needed and attach between the supports, the bottom one about 2 in. above the top of the bottom leg and the upper one about 15 in. above the top of the bottom leg. (The exact locations do not matter, as long as they are square to the uprights.)

18 To make the back slats, rip-cut a 1×8 in half (for pieces about 3½ in. wide) and cut five slats 30 in. long. Rout all edges that are not already rounded over.

19 Position the back slats on a flat surface with ¼-in. spacers between. Measure the width; they should either fit perfectly between the bottom legs or you should plan to notch the slats when you install them. Use a long compass as shown to mark a curve with a 25-in. radius across the boards near their tops.

20 Cut the curved lines with a jigsaw. Rout the tops and all edges that are not already rounded, and sand as needed for a neat appearance.

21 Attach the center back slat so its top is about 3 in. above the back uprights. Measure carefully to center it between the uprights, and attach by drilling pilot/counterbore holes, adding dabs of polyurethane construction adhesive, and driving screws.

tip

The bottom of the back slats could be cut in a neat line, but since they will not show it's fine for them to be in a somewhat ragged line.

22 Attach the other back slats with pilot/ counterbore holes and screws. You may find it easier to install these with the chair leaning on its back. In our example, the outer slats were very slightly notched to fit against the bottom legs.

23 Rip-cut a 1×8 board in thirds to produce seat slats that are about 2⅜ in. wide. Cut the slats to span across the bottom legs, so they fit snugly between the front legs. Rout and sand all the slats for a neat appearance.

24 Line the seat slats up and drill pilot holes for screws that will drive into the centers of the bottom legs. Arrange the seat slats on the bottom legs with spacers; the front-most slat can overhang the bottom seat by as much as 1¼ in. Add dabs of polyurethane adhesive to the under- sides of the slats and drive screws to attach.

25 Use the pattern on p. 108 or make a design of your own to cut two arm rest supports. Rout and sand all edges except for the long straight edge. Attach to the sides of the front legs, the tops flush with the tops of the front legs.

27 Fill the screw holes. Here we chose decorative "button plugs" for the areas that don't need to be smooth: Add a drop of wood glue to the plug (or to the hole) and tap it in with a hammer.

26 Attach the arm rests by drilling pilot/counterbore holes and driving screws vertically down into the arm rest supports and the front legs; also drive screws horizontally into the back uprights.

28 The seat back and the front part of the arm rests need to be smooth, so we used a plug cutter to make plugs, added wood glue, tapped them in, and sanded when the glue dried (see p. 37). Sand and apply stain and sealer or primer and paint.

Adirondack Ottoman

This project not only has a name that fairly trips off the tongue (you could call it an "Adirondack Footstool" instead, but that's much less lyrical), it also provides extra comfort for Adirondack-style lounging. Without much trouble, you can build it to fit perfectly against your chair, for a seamless transition and lots of leg comfort. Once in place the chair and ottoman look like a single piece of furniture—a sort of chaise lounge. Yet the ottoman is so light that it can be easily scooted to the side if you like.

We use cedar, which is easy to work with, lightweight, resistant to rot, and good looking to boot. As with the chair, routed slat edges are on prominent display, so it pays to spend time getting your roundover bit precisely adjusted, and to do a little practicing on scrap pieces.

MATERIALS

- two 8-ft. cedar 1×8s, for all pieces
- 1⅝-in. stainless-steel or decking screws
- polyurethane construction adhesive, with caulk gun
- wood plugs (plus plugs that you cut yourself)
- stain and sealer, or primer and paint

TOOLS

- chopsaw
- tablesaw or circular saw
- jigsaw
- trammel (long compass) made of cardboard, screw, and pencil
- belt sander
- router with roundover bit
- wood plane or surform tool
- hand sanding block
- large square
- drill with screwdriver, pilot/counterbore, and plug-cutting bits

ADIRONDACK OTTOMAN

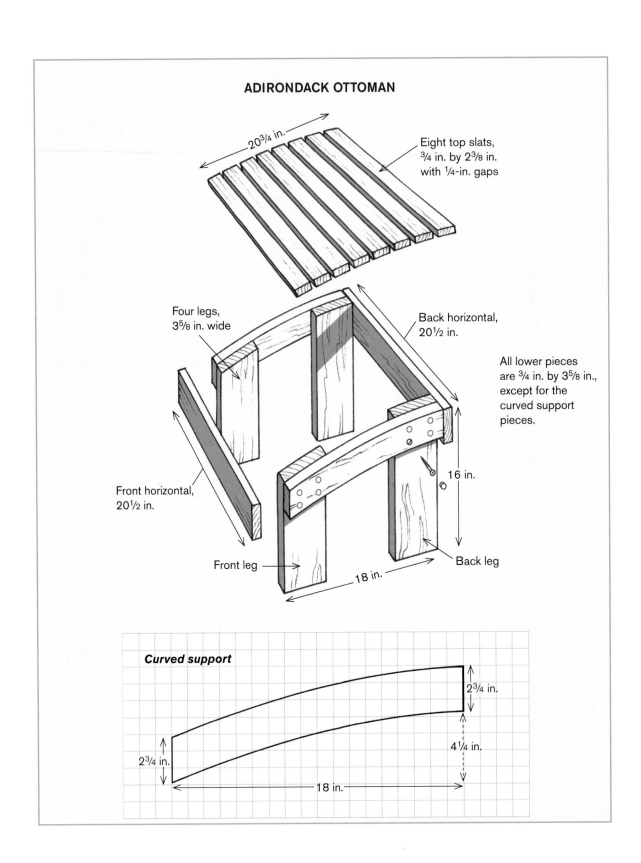

20¾ in.

Eight top slats,
¾ in. by 2⅜ in.
with ¼-in. gaps

Four legs,
3⅝ in. wide

Back horizontal,
20½ in.

All lower pieces
are ¾ in. by 3⅝ in.,
except for the
curved support
pieces.

Front horizontal,
20½ in.

16 in.

Front leg

Back leg

18 in.

Curved support

2¾ in.

2¾ in.

4¼ in.

18 in.

1 Rip-cut a 1×8 board in thirds to produce pieces that are about 2⅜ in. wide. You will cut the top slats out of these. From the other 1×8, cut off two 18-in.-long pieces to be used for the curved supports. Rip the remaining piece in half, to make pieces about 3⅝ in. wide.

2 Cut eight top slats to the same length as those on the Adirondack chair it will accompany—in our case, 21 in. Cut two of the 3⅝-in.-wide pieces to 20½ in. long (so the top slats overhang slightly on each side) for the front and back horizontals.

3 To make a curved support, use a trammel, as shown. Place the cardboard strip so it is square to the board at one end. Drive a screw 36 in. from the top of the board, poke a pencil through the cardboard 2¾ in. down from the top of the board, and draw the bottom line. Move the compass up 2¾ in. and draw a parallel top line. Cut the piece at both lines and use it as a template to mark the other curved piece.

4 Belt-sand the curved pieces to achieve smooth arcs. Lightly sand the edges, but do not rout.

5 To build the frame, drill pilot/counterbore holes and drive screws to attach the front and back horizontals from step 2 to the faces of the curved pieces.

6 The front horizontal piece needs to be planed down so the top slats can form a continuously curved surface. Use a wood plane, as shown, or use a surform tool, to remove the material.

7 In order to make an ottoman that is the same height as the chair, measure the height of the chair's frame at the front of the chair, as shown, and cut the ottoman's back legs to the same height.

tip

When planing, take time to adjust the blade to just the right depth, so it removes shavings with easy pressure, without snagging on the wood. If you have trouble planing in one direction, try going in the other direction.

tip

When assembling a frame like this, it helps to screw a scrap board onto the table, so you can press the assembly against it as you drill and drive screws.

8 Rout the bottom ends of the back legs, as well as the sides that are not already rounded. Position a back leg against the back horizontal piece, on the inside of the frame. (There is no way to check this for square, since the support piece is curved.) Drill pilot/counterbore holes and drive four screws to attach each back leg.

9 Hold the frame against the Adirondack chair and raise the frame until it pleasingly follows the arc of the chair's seat. Clamp a front leg piece in this position and scribe a cut line, as shown.

10 Cut the front leg with a jigsaw and use it as a template for marking the other front leg. Rout the unrounded edges as well as the bottom end. Press each front leg against the front horizontal piece and drive four screws to attach.

11 Place all the top slats on a flat surface with their ends aligned. Measure and mark for screw holes in a straight line; position them so the screws will drive into the centers of the curved supports. Drill pilot/counterbore holes.

12 Position the lowest slat so it slightly overhangs the frame evenly, and drive screws, where you've marked, to attach it. Position the remaining slats, with spacers. Use a straight board to align the slats with each other.

13 Remove the slats and squirt a bead of polyurethane adhesive onto the curved support. Continually checking for straight alignment, drive screws to attach the slats to the frame. The top piece can overhang by as much as an inch.

14 Cut plugs out of the same wood as the ottoman, add drops of wood glue, and tap the plugs into the holes. Allow to dry, then sand smooth with a hand sanding block (see p. 43). Apply stain and sealer, or primer and paint.

Adirondack Table

This project is the third and final piece of the Adirondack ensemble, giving you a trio of coordinating pieces that will come together in harmony. Where the ottoman uses narrow slats like those on the chair's seat, this table uses slats just as wide as those on the chair's back—giving the trio a nice sense of symmetry. With these three pieces in your yard your time outdoors is sure to be restful and comfortable.

As with the chair and the ottoman, cedar is used here for its beauty, ease of working, and resistance to rot. The top is made of cedar 1-by, while all the other parts are made of 5/4×6 cedar decking. The two stretchers, plus the 18-in.-long feet, make this a very stable table even though it feels a bit airy with its two legs.

MATERIALS

- two 8-ft. cedar 5/4×6 decking
- one 6-ft. cedar 1×8
- 1⅝-in. and 1¼-in. stainless-steel or decking screws
- polyurethane construction adhesive, with caulk gun
- wood plugs (plus plugs that you cut yourself)
- exterior wood glue
- stain and sealer, or primer and paint

TOOLS

- chopsaw
- tablesaw or circular saw
- jigsaw
- compass
- utility knife
- trammel (long compass) made of cardboard, screw, and pencil
- belt sander
- router with roundover bit
- hand sanding block
- large square
- drill with screwdriver, pilot/counterbore, and plug-cutting bits
- chisel

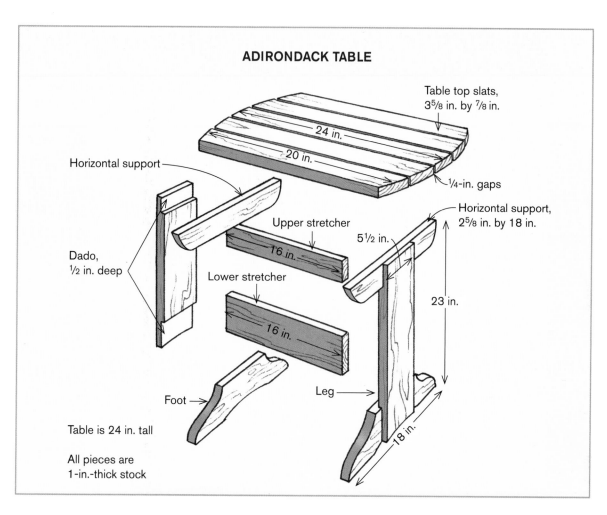

ADIRONDACK TABLE

Table top slats, 3⅝ in. by ⅞ in.

24 in.

20 in.

¼-in. gaps

Horizontal support

Upper stretcher

16 in.

5½ in.

Horizontal support, 2⅝ in. by 18 in.

Dado, ½ in. deep

Lower stretcher

16 in.

23 in.

Foot

Leg

18 in.

Table is 24 in. tall

All pieces are 1-in.-thick stock

1 Rip the 1×8 in half to make two pieces 3⅝ in. wide. From these pieces cut five pieces 24 in. long for the top slats. Cut 4 ft. from one of the decking pieces. Rip this 4-ft.-long piece in half to make pieces about 2⅝ in. wide. Cut one of them 16 in. long for the upper stretcher.

2 From the remaining 2⅝-in.-wide pieces cut two horizontal supports 18 in. long. Use a compass to mark the ends of the horizontal supports for curve cuts, cut with a jigsaw, then rout the edges and hand sand.

3 From the full-width board cut two pieces 18 in. long for the feet. On one of the boards make small marks 5 in. from each side. Position a 5-gal. bucket against the two marks and draw a curved cut line. Cut the line with a jigsaw.

4 Use two plates (or other round objects of your choice) to draw an S-curve on a top corner of the foot. Before cutting, experiment on scrap pieces to achieve a look you like. Cut the S-curve with a jigsaw.

5 Use the cutout as a template to mark the other side of the foot and cut with a jigsaw. Use a belt sander to smooth out the curves, then use the first foot as a template for marking the second foot. Cut it as well.

6 Equip a router with a roundover bit and adjust and test on scrap pieces until it rounds edges to look like factory-rounded decking edges. Rout all the cut lines.

tip

As the photo for step 6 shows, you can place a board next to the piece you are routing, to help ensure against wobbling as you rout.

7 From the remaining full-width board cut two legs 23 in. long. On each, place a horizontal support at one end and a foot at the other end. Use small boards to align these pieces with the leg's ends. Measure to be sure that the foot is centered on the leg, then scribe a line that follows the foot's lower curve. Also scribe a line at the top of the foot, as well as a line that follows the bottom of the horizontal support.

8 On each leg cut the bottom curved line with a jigsaw. Belt sand, rout, and hand sand the curved cuts.

9 Set your circular saw's blade depth to ½ in., the depth of the dado you will cut in the top and bottom of the leg. Following the steps on pp. 41–42, slit the outside pencil marks you made in step 7 with a utility knife to prevent tearout, then cut a series of closely spaced kerfs.

tip

When cutting kerfs for a dado, be sure to keep the saw's base plate flat on the board as you work. If you wobble near the end, you will cut too deeply.

10 Tap the wood slivers with a hammer, then use a chisel to scrape away all the protrusions. Finish with the chisel's bevel side down, as shown. Do this completely; even one little bump can make the joint sloppy looking. To do this with a router, see p. 97.

11 Place the dado-cut leg on top of the foot and the horizontal support and check that the joint looks tight; if not, clean out the dado more thoroughly. Apply polyurethane adhesive to each joint, then drill pilot holes and drive four widely spaced 1¼-in. screws into each joint. Check for square as you work. Repeat for the other leg.

12 The lower stretcher rests on the top of the feet; the upper stretcher butts up against the bottom of the horizontal supports. From the outside of each leg measure and mark the locations for the pilot holes, centered on the leg—three for the bottom stretcher and two for the upper stretcher. Drill the pilot holes using a pilot/counterbore bit.

13 Position the bottom stretcher on top of the feet and centered on the legs and drive screws to attach it to both legs. Then attach the upper stretcher also centered on the legs as shown.

14 Lay the top slats on the horizontal supports and use nails or thin strips of wood to keep them evenly spaced. Drill pilot/counterbore holes, then drive screws to attach.

15 Make a trammel out of a strip of cardboard, a screw, and a pencil, as shown. Partially drive the screw through the cardboard and into the center of the center slat, near its end, and draw a curved line on the other end. Repeat for the other side.

16 Cut the curved lines with a jigsaw. Then use a belt sander to shape a more perfect curve; go over the edge with a router with a roundover bit.

17 Use a drill with a plug-cutting bit to make wood plugs, insert them with drops of wood glue, and allow to dry. Then scrape nearly smooth with a sharp chisel. Hand sand the surface of the table so the plugs are smooth and on the same plane as the slats. Apply stain and sealer, or primer and paint.

Dining Table

This dining table has chunky, straightforward framing in a rough Mission sort of style, made with 4×4s and 2×4s. The tabletop is made of slate tile that is framed with oak.

There are a number of ways you could vary the design without much complication. You could opt for different wood and different stain. Ipé is a common choice for the tabletop; the white oak we chose is almost as resistant to rot and about half the price. Our table is 40 in. by 50 in., about average for a table that seats six; you could lengthen or shorten the table by a foot or so. If you make it longer, install a middle support for the table top.

(continued on p. 130)

MATERIALS

- one 6-ft. pressure-treated 4×4
- three 8-ft. pressure-treated 2×4s
- sheet of ¾-in. pressure-treated plywood, about 40 in. by 50 in.
- 5/4×6 oak: two pieces at 8 ft., one piece at 4 ft.
- one sheet of ¼-in. or ½-in. backer board (thickness depends on the thickness of the tiles)
- fourteen 12-in. slate tiles (you only need twelve, but one or two might break or be miscut)
- four 8-in.-long ⅜-in. lag screws, with washers
- eight 6-in.-long ⅜-in. lag screws, with washers
- 2½-in., 1¼-in., and 1-in. deck screws
- polyurethane construction adhesive, with caulk gun
- one bag polymer-fortified thinset mortar
- small box of fortified grout
- stain and sealer; for this project we used satin polyurethane
- masonry sealer

TOOLS

- chopsaw or circular saw
- tablesaw or circular saw
- drill with screwdriver, 5/16-in. bit, and a long ¼-in. bit
- long clamps
- pocket-screw kit with screws
- utility knife
- square
- impact driver with bit for driving the lag screws, or a ratchet and socket
- backer board cutter and straightedge
- wet tile cutter
- square-notched trowel, grout float, and large sponge

DINING TABLE FRAME

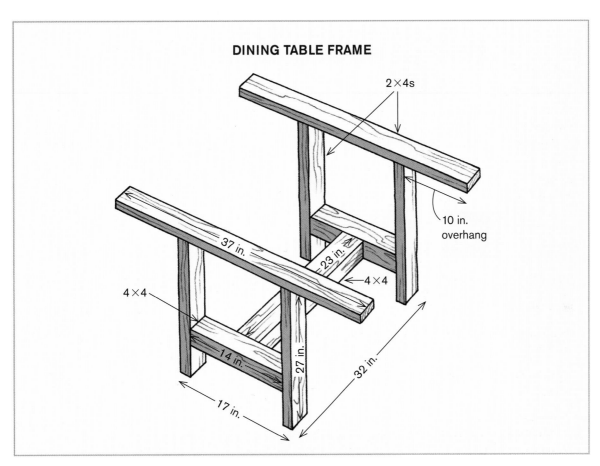

2×4s

10 in. overhang

37 in.

23 in.

4×4

4×4

14 in.

27 in.

17 in.

32 in.

DETAIL OF DINING TABLE TOP

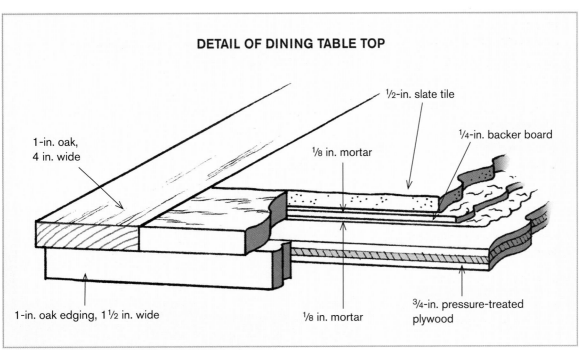

1-in. oak, 4 in. wide

1-in. oak edging, 1½ in. wide

⅛ in. mortar

⅛ in. mortar

½-in. slate tile

¼-in. backer board

¾-in. pressure-treated plywood

We've chosen to join the lower frame with exposed bolt heads with washers, for a rustic look; you may want to sink and plug the screw heads instead.

The table top combines hardwood with extremely inexpensive natural slate tiles. These tiles are often soft and easily broken, but will last for decades if set in a firm bed of mortar and backer board and maintained with twice-yearly applications of ma-sonry sealer. For a more maintenance-free surface, perhaps choose granite or porcelain tiles.

We built the frame using pressure-treated wood, which can be dark-stained to look much like the table top's wood, at least from a distance. If you use a lighter stain, you may opt for cedar or redwood, or even ipé, instead.

1 Cut the pieces for the frame: two 4×4 pieces at 14 in. long; one 4×4 piece at 23 in. long; four 2×4 pieces at 27 in. long; and two 2×4 pieces at 37 in. long (see the drawing on p. 129).

2 Lay the I-shaped 4×4 assembly, consisting of the two 14-in. 4×4s at the ends with the 23-in. 4×4 in the middle, with the worst-looking sides of the boards facing down. On the short pieces, draw square lines indicating the location of the long stretcher, and continue the lines down the face. Using these lines for reference, mark the locations for two diagonally arranged lag screws, 1 in. down from the top or bottom and 1 in. inside the lines.

3 Place the short 4×4 on a pair of blocks and drill down through it at the two marked locations with a ⁵⁄₁₆-in. bit. Turn the board over and use a utility knife to cut away any protrusions, which would interfere with making a tight joint. Repeat for the other short 4×4.

4 Mark the long ¼-in. bit with a piece of tape indicating how deep you will drill. You should drill about ½ in. deeper than the length of the 8-in. screw. Clamp the three pieces together in correct alignment. (Position the clamp so you can drill through both holes.) Drill through the holes you made in step 3 with the long bit, pulling it out several times to release sawdust.

5 Slip washers onto the 8-in. lag screws and drive them into the holes. Use an impact driver (shown) if you have one. If not, use a socket wrench.

6 Place the I-shaped 4×4 section on top of two 4×4 blocks, and place a 2×4 leg against the end of one of the short pieces. Use a square to mark reference lines, then mark for the locations of two diagonally arranged screw holes, 1 in. away from the board's edge and 1 in. away from the reference line. Mark all four legs in the same way. Drill through the marked locations with the ⁵⁄₁₆-in. bit.

7 Clamp a pair of legs in position on both sides of one of the short 4×4s. Check that the legs are square to the 4×4 in both directions. Mark the long ¼-in. bit with tape for a hole that is ½ in. deeper than the 6-in. screws you will drive. Drill the holes, then drive the screws with an impact driver or socket wrench.

> **tip**
>
> If the oak board used for the frame of the table top has a rough edge or two, smooth it using a hand plane (or power plane, if you have one), then a belt sander. Lightly hand sand the edge corners to make them less sharp.

8 Center one of the 37-in. 2×4s over the legs and drive deck screws to attach it. Repeat with the other 37-in. 2×4. Now the table's frame is complete.

9 Rip-cut 5/4 oak (which is about 5½ in. wide) to produce one piece that is about 4 in. wide and one that is 1½ in. wide. The narrow piece will be used as the edging, below the wider piece (step 13). Cut the pieces to length to produce a frame that is 40 in. by 50 in. when butt-jointed. (For the long pieces, subtract the width of two of the short pieces.)

10 To join the butt-jointed oak boards that will frame the table top, use pocket screws, which join the boards from underneath (see p. 42). Use a jig made for ¾-in. to 1-in. boards. To adjust for the depth of the hole, slip in the drill bit, resting it on a nickel at the bottom, and tighten the stop collar. Clamp the jig to the bottom of the board and drill the holes.

11 Clamp the four boards together. Tap with a hammer and block of wood to ensure a perfect fit, and drive the screws. Cut and attach a middle piece in the same way.

tip

On a project like this you probably want to select just the right color of stain. So experiment: Paint sections of a scrap piece of the wood, the same type you will use in your project, with various stains. Allow the stains to dry if you plan to coat with a sealer. Once dry apply sealer as well, because it will change the color slightly. Set the samples board next to the tiles and make your selection.

12 The plywood that the hardwood frame rests on (see the illustration on p. 129) must allow room for the thickness of the underhanging edging plus a ¼-in. overhang. If the edging is 1 in. thick, scribe a line all around the underside of the hardwood frame, 1¼ in. from the outer edge. Measure the space between those lines and cut plywood to fit.

13 Test the fit of the plywood and recut if needed. Apply beads of polyurethane construction adhesive to the hardwood frame and set the plywood on top. Adjust so the plywood is 1¼ in. away from the edges at all points, and drive 1¼-in. screws to attach. Cut the 1½-in-wide oak strips (from step 9) to length and attach with pilot holes and screws.

tip
Before you drive the pocket screws, remember that it is the underside (which is actually the top) that will show. If your hardwood boards are slightly unequal in thickness (as sometimes happens), gently lift up the boards and check that they are on the same plane underneath.

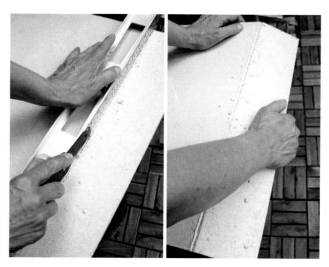

tip

If the 1¼-in. screws do not grab tightly but spin instead, drill pilot holes through the plywood only and not the hardwood; that will help them hold tight. (You could use 1⅝-in. screws, but then you run the risk of poking through the hardwood if you sink the heads.)

14 Attach the table top to the frame. We've chosen to drive screws from underneath so the top can be removed later to make it easier to move. Apply stain and allow to dry. Then apply satin polyurethane or other sealer and allow it to dry as well.

15 Cut two pieces of backer board to fit in the hardwood frame. Measure the openings and subtract ¼ in. (because the cut edges get pretty ragged). Use a backer-board cutter and a straight-edge to score along the line; make several passes. Then snap the board with your hands.

tip

The thickness of the backer-board sheet you use depends on the thickness of your tiles. The thickness of the backer board, the mortar, and the tiles should equal or be slightly thicker than the edging boards. These slate tiles vary in thickness, and some are pretty thick, so we've chosen to use ¼-in. backer board, which means that the mortar will need to be pretty thick in places.

16 Mix a batch of polymer-fortified thinset mortar according to the directions. Carefully drop dollops on the exposed plywood centers of the frame and use a square-notched trowel to spread it evenly. Set the backer board in the mortar and drive a grid of 1-in. screws spaced 6 in. apart.

17 Lay the tiles out in a pleasing arrangement and mark for cuts, leaving ⅛-in. gaps between the tiles. Cut the tile with a wet-cutting tile saw. (If you install ceramic tile, you can use a snap cutter.)

18 Dry-lay the tiles to make sure they are all cut correctly. Remove them and trowel a layer of thinset mortar onto the backer board. The thickness of the thinset depends on the thickness of the tiles; you want them to end up at the same height as the wood frame. Set the tiles in the mortar. In our case many of the thinner tiles had to be back-buttered with additional mortar to bring them up to the right height. Another method is to add dollops of mortar, which make it easier to push one side down to the correct height.

19 Natural stone tiles will soak up grout, making for a very difficult cleaning job after grouting. To prevent this, apply masonry sealer to the tops (not the edges) of the tiles and allow to dry.

tip

When working with mortar, do your best to keep things clean. Trowel carefully and wipe up any spills immediately. We chose to keep the wood uncovered because it was well sealed, but you may choose to cover it with painter's tape and paper.

20 Mix a batch of fortified grout according to the directions. Spread it with a grout float, holding the float nearly flat and moving in several directions to force the grout into the joints at all points. Always hold the float at an angle to the joint lines to avoid digging in and removing too much grout.

21 Tip the float up and scrape away as much grout as you can. Again, hold the float at an angle to avoid digging into the joints.

22 Wipe with a damp sponge, continually rinsing it in a bucket of water, changing the water when it gets dirty. As you wipe, work to achieve grout joints that are consistent in height. You'll need to wipe three or four times. Allow the grout to dry, then buff the surface with a dry cloth to remove all grout residue from the surface of the tile. Reapply masonry sealer, and touch up the wood finish as needed.

Tree Bench

A tree bench is not (as some may assume) a bench made out of a tree, but a bench that wraps around a tree. It makes a lovely decorative frame around a favorite tree and offers an inviting place to sit. As the author's young adult children have pointed out, it is semi-social, since its shape encourages people to look away from each other. For that reason, it could possibly be thought of as a "texting bench."

Ideally, the tree should be mid-sized—say, 16 in. to 30 in. in diameter, large enough so people have something to rest their backs against. But you may choose to build a bench around a smaller tree as proof that you believe in the future; the family will enjoy watching the tree's trunk expand closer and closer to the bench over the years, and if you take photos by the tree you may be able to guess the year by gauging the size of the tree.

If the ground around the tree is fairly level, it will make building easier. But many trees have sloped sites or roots that protrude up from the ground, and that should not keep you from building. Legs can be shortened or lengthened, or small holes can be dug in the soil to compensate for unevenness. And keep in mind that your bench doesn't need to be perfectly level.

The bench shown is made entirely of pressure-treated decking that is extra thick—about 1¼ in.—but standard 1-in.-thick decking would work as well, as would 2×6s We applied a coat of stain to this lumber, but you may choose to paint instead.

MATERIALS

- ☐ 5/4×6 treated or cedar decking (for this project with a 24-in.-diameter tree, we used seven 12-ft. boards)

- ☐ 2-in. decking screws

TOOLS

- ☐ chopsaw

- ☐ level

- ☐ hand sanding block

- ☐ drill with screwdriver and pilot/counterbore bits

- ☐ circular saw or reciprocating saw

- ☐ large square

- ☐ shovel

- ☐ angle square

TREE BENCH

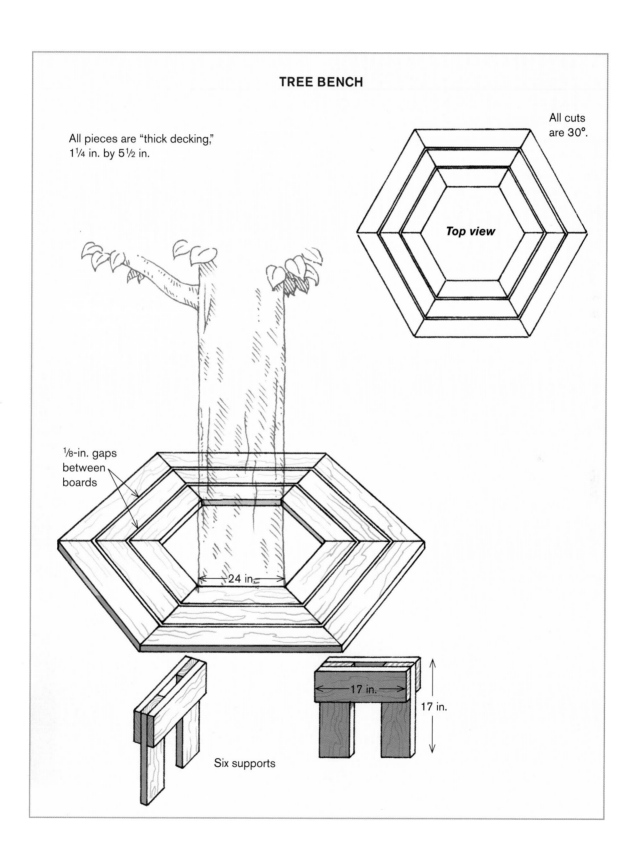

All pieces are "thick decking," 1¼ in. by 5½ in.

All cuts are 30°.

Top view

⅛-in. gaps between boards

24 in.

17 in.

17 in.

Six supports

1 Measure the diameter of the tree at its widest point at 17 in. above the ground. (Most tree trunks are slightly oval rather than perfectly round.) If you have a mature tree that grows slowly, make this measurement the inside (shorter) dimension for the boards nearest the tree. If you have a fast-growing tree, add two or three inches.

tip

If you are unsure when measuring a trunk's diameter, instead measure around the trunk for the circumference. (A metal tape measure works pretty well for this, but a dressmaker's cloth measure is more accurate.) Now recall 8th-grade math: Divide the circumference by pi (3.14) to get the diameter. If the trunk is visibly oval rather than circular, add a few inches.

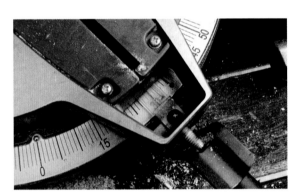

2 Set a chopsaw to cut at 30 degrees. It is possible to make these cuts with a circular saw, but it is a good deal more difficult.

3 It's best to keep the saw at the same position, rather than constantly switching from side to side between cuts. Make the first cut, then flip the board over and mark for the cut on the other side.

4 Because the chopsaw's blade will start cutting in the middle of the board, use an angle square to mark a 30-degree line before making the second cut. Make the cut, then use the first piece as a template to mark the other five boards.

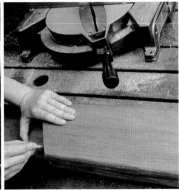

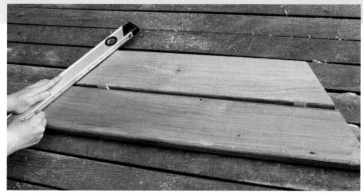

5 To cut the next (middle) row of boards, cut one side of a long board at 30 degrees. Line it up with a first-row board on a flat surface as shown, with spacers between the boards. Use a straightedge to make sure they are perfectly aligned on the side that is already cut. Then use a straightedge to mark the next board for cutting. Cut this and five other boards to this size, then use the same method to measure for the third row and cut six of those as well.

6 Use a hand sanding block to ease (slightly bevel) the cut edges. This will help hide imperfections in the joints, which inevitably occur in a project like this.

7 Use a level and a tape measure to measure the ground's slope around your tree. Eyeball the area to look for high places where you might be able to dig small holes (step 15). If digging is not a possibility and the slope is more than a few inches, plan to make some of the legs a few inches longer than others.

8 Line the boards up on a flat lawn or driveway. Measure to find the best length for the supports. (This can vary, because decking boards can vary in width.) In our example a support that is 3 in. thick and 17 in. long will work well.

9 Our supports will also be 17 in. tall, which means that all four pieces of each support are 17 in. Some serious gang-cutting is in order. Screw the chopsaw to a table and attach a simple stop, as shown, so you can simply slide the boards into position to get the same dimension for each cut. You will need 24 pieces.

10 Use a square to keep things aligned, and a scrap piece to hold the legs up, as you build each of the six supports. Use an angle square (inset) to make sure the tops of the horizontals are even with each other. Drive four widely spaced screws into each joint, on each side.

11 Working on a flat surface, start assembling; this is much easier with a helper or two. Place boards for two sections so their joints are centered over a support; on the two outside sides, the supports do not have to be correctly aligned at this point. Slip in spacers and work to make the joints tight and centered on the support.

12 Once you are happy with the arrangement, drill pilot holes and drive screws to attach the boards to the horizontal supports.

tip

After you get going it's a good idea to mass-produce pilot holes in all the boards prior to assembly, since they are all spaced $1\frac{1}{2}$ in. away from the cut edges.

13 Assemble three sections in this way, to make the first half of the bench. Continually check that spacing between boards is consistent (though you may abandon the spacers after a while), and aim for tight joints. Finish by attaching the boards at both ends to one side of the supports (above right).

14 Working with a helper or two, carefully carry the first half of the bench to the tree and place it so it is evenly spaced away from the trunk. Wherever possible, adjust its position to avoid placing supports on roots or any high or low spots.

15 Check the bench for level; you don't need to be perfect, but close is good. If a support is high, you may be able to dig a small hole and lower it. If you cannot dig a hole, use a circular saw or a reciprocating saw to cut a support near the bottom.

16 Build the other half of the bench. This one has three seat sections, but only two supports. Use buckets and boards, as shown, or chairs to hold up the unsupported ends as you work.

17 Very carefully carry the second half over to the tree. On each side, use a board to hold all three unsupported board ends as you carry. Position the bench and place the ends on the supports that are attached to the first half.

18 Drill pilot holes and drive screws to attach the second-half board ends. Before or after doing this, you may need to dig holes or cut leg bottoms to make the bench fairly level and to produce good-looking joints.

5 bamboo projects

ADD A UNIQUE decorative touch to your back-yard with a simple bamboo structure or even a few bamboo structures. Often when people think of bamboo they think of a Japanese or Chinese garden, and it's certainly true that bamboo can make a place feel a bit Asian-inspired. But at least one species of bamboo (sometimes called "river cane" or "switch cane") is native to the American South, and the bamboo fishin' pole is as American as apple pie. So an occasional bamboo structure may fit in well amid rustic-looking wood planters and trellises.

Bamboo (which is biologically a grass rather than a wood) is in many ways amazingly strong. In other countries it is commonly used as a serious construction material, even supporting poured upper-story concrete floors. However, it is also prone to cracking, so building techniques differ from those used for wood.

In this chapter we'll demonstrate some simple and attractive ways to fasten bamboo. We'll take a pass on trying to show methods used by skilled bamboo craftsmen, who can create tight joints that are similar to mortise-and-tenon joints, often using only a machete or a knife. Instead, our methods can be learned quickly and easily. In some cases we "cheat" by driving a screw where it can't be seen, then wrapping with Bonsai wire or twine for an authentic look.

Bamboo Materials, Tools, and Techniques

With a bit of knowledge about bamboo, a few simple tools, and some techniques that you can learn in an hour, you can soon build basic bamboo projects.

CHOOSING BAMBOO

Though an unusual material, bamboo is actually available most anywhere. In many areas, local hardware stores, home centers, or plant nurseries carry selections of bamboo poles in various thicknesses. If there are no such sources near you, you can go online and order bamboo poles, slats, woven mats, and fencing panels.

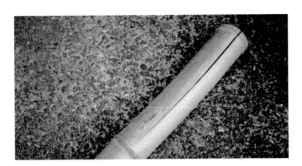

When choosing bamboo poles, you will probably look for those that are free of splits. However, thin splits like the one seen here are more cosmetic than structural: As long as you don't do anything to stress the pole, it will be strong enough for most outdoor projects.

There are hundreds of bamboo species, each with slightly different colors and characteristics. For construction purposes, bamboo is often broken down into two types: Tonkin and Moso. Tonkin is generally less than 2 in. in diameter, is tan in color, and has smooth nodes. Moso bamboo is generally larger and tends to be less straight than Tonkin. Its nodes are also more closely spaced than those of Tonkin. If you are given a choice between the two, go for Moso if you want extra strength or a rougher appearance, and use Tonkin for a cleaner, straighter look.

When possible, cut bamboo close to the nodes, like this, so the ends will be strong.

MATERIALS AND TOOLS
Special tools and materials may be available at specialty stores in your area; if not, you can get all the stuff you'll need from online sources. Some projects require only carpentry tools plus either bonsai wire or twine.

Bonsai wire is black and easy to work with, enabling a beginner to produce great-looking joints that hold well with only a small amount of practice. It comes in various thicknesses; for most small projects 1.0mm, 1.5mm, and 2.0mm thicknesses will give you enough options. For a traditional look use twine; palm rope (shown) is a popular choice. Unless you are very good at knot tying, don't expect to make reliable joints with twine alone; use it in conjunction with screws.

safety tip

Bamboo can be cut using a handsaw or a power saw. Be aware that cutting with a power tool throws off sharp shavings rather than fine sawdust, so wear a dust mask and eye protection.

To really get into the spirit of things you may want to buy some traditional bamboo tools. From top to bottom: A bamboo hatchet easily splits bamboo in half. A gyokucho saw has fine teeth that are just right for cutting bamboo without splitting. A bamboo splitter divides a bamboo pole into three, four, six, or even eight slats. And a Mikihisa knife is made of high-carbon steel and is beveled on only one side, so you can more cleanly remove small branches.

A FEW TECHNIQUES

Many of these techniques will also be demonstrated in the following projects, but here are a few handy tips.

Joining with screws. Though some may consider it cheating, joining bamboo with screws is often the best way to create a durable joint. But because bamboo splits easily and is hollow, some special methods ensure the screw will grab firmly without cracking a pole.

tip

If you are joining a small-diameter pole to another pole, simply hold the two pieces together, drill a pilot hole of the right size (see step 1), and drive the screw.

Unless you like the way they look, cut small branches off flush with the node for a more finished look.

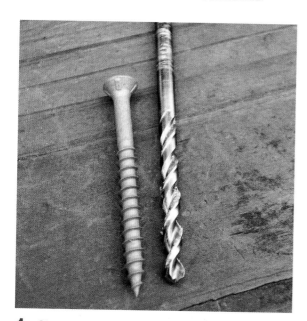

1 Choose the drill bit carefully. It should be just slightly thinner than the screw, or the bamboo will crack. Test on scrap pieces to make sure the screw will grab.

2 Drill a hole through one of the pieces to be joined. Aim to bore through the center of the pole. Hold the first pole in place against the second and drill through the second on only one side—not all the way through.

3 Drive the screw through the first hole. Then, you will often need to guide it toward the second hole; it won't go there automatically.

4 Drive the screw so it pokes through the first pole by 1/8 in. or so. Insert the tip of the screw into the second pole's hole. Drive the screw, but not too hard: Take care to stop driving once the head meets the bamboo, or it may crack.

Finishing bamboo. New bamboo has a shiny surface that resists staining or sealing. Most often, bamboo is not stained or sealed but is allowed to mellow out. Depending on your climate, a bamboo project may last only 10 years. For longer life you may want to apply a sealer. To do so, first rub the bamboo with steel wool or hand-held sandpaper to remove the finish. Or wait a year or so for the gloss to wear off, then apply finish. Use a high-quality penetrating sealer, a semi-transparent stain, or tung oil. If the finish material beads up, then you know the area needs to be sanded more before finishing.

Bamboo and the ground. Bamboo will not survive long if in contact with soil unless the soil is very dry most of the time. Rather than driving bamboo poles into the ground, first pound in a stake made of rot-resistant wood or metal, and tie the bamboo to the stake.

This splitter divides a fairly thick bamboo pole into three slats. To make the split, center the splitter on the pole's end and bang with a piece of bamboo or a wood mallet.

Simple Bamboo Trellis

Even a straightforward trellis made from bamboo poles will have a handmade charm that brightens up a garden space. A bamboo trellis with a square or rectangular grid usually looks better than one with an angled grid. For this project we've made the joints using only bonsai wire, which stays strong if wrapped tightly. For added strength you could first drill pilot holes and drive small screws through the back. Then wrap with wire or twine for a traditional look and a little more holding power. Here we use ¾-in. poles spaced 8 in. apart; you may choose different sizes and spacing.

MATERIALS

- ☐ bamboo poles (for the project shown, about a dozen 5-ft. and 8-ft. poles were used)
- ☐ bonsai wire
- ☐ wood or metal stakes

TOOLS

- ☐ handsaw or loppers for cutting poles
- ☐ lineman's pliers
- ☐ framing square

1 Use a handsaw to cut the bamboo poles to the desired lengths. For small poles you can use a pair of garden loppers. Roughly lay out the job to get an overall idea. It helps to work against a wall or other straightedge.

2 As you work, use a framing square to see that the poles are at least roughly square to each other. Cut a piece of bamboo or wood to act as a spacer; the one we use here is 8 in. long. Before making each connection, check that the opening is correct in both directions. You won't achieve perfection, but you should aim for it.

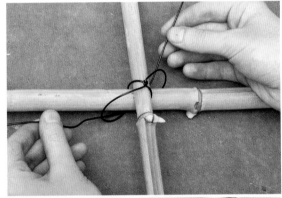

3 To make a simple joint with wire, slip the wire under the two pieces and pull up to see that the ends are equal in length. Holding the wires taut, twist them a three-quarter turn. The joint should feel fairly tight.

tip

In this project we show a simple way of tying with wire. For a somewhat more complex approach, see the fan trellis (p. 157).

4 Slip the wires under the bamboo so they run at the other angle. Pull them taut.

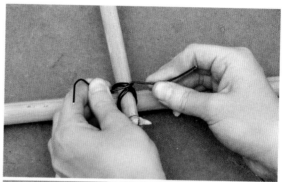

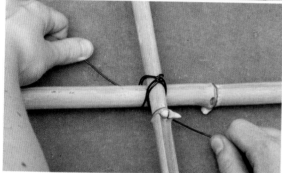

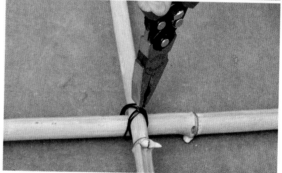

5 Twist again a three-quarter turn, then slip the wires under again.

6 Twist a last time by hand. Then use lineman's pliers to twist more tightly. When using the lineman's pliers make sure to snug the knot, but don't overtighten or the wire will break.

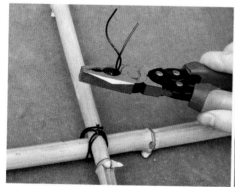

7 Snip off the excess wire, then push the wires down. To install in your garden, simply lean the trellis in place or attach it to a stake with wire.

Bamboo Tripod

A bamboo tripod can be dropped most anywhere in a garden or flowerbed. You can train vines to crawl up it, you can hook a small hanging plant from its top knot, or it can just sit there to provide a focal point or visual frame.

This is perhaps the simplest project in the book. Still, it calls for a bit of knack and some practice to achieve a knot that is neatly wrapped with no crossing over. There are three basic components of the knot: a clove hitch on the first pole, wrapping around the other poles, and "frapping"—wrapping sideways to tighten the whole knot assemblage.

MATERIALS

- **three bamboo poles, the same length and about the same thickness**

- **bonsai wire or twine**

TOOLS

- **lineman's pliers**

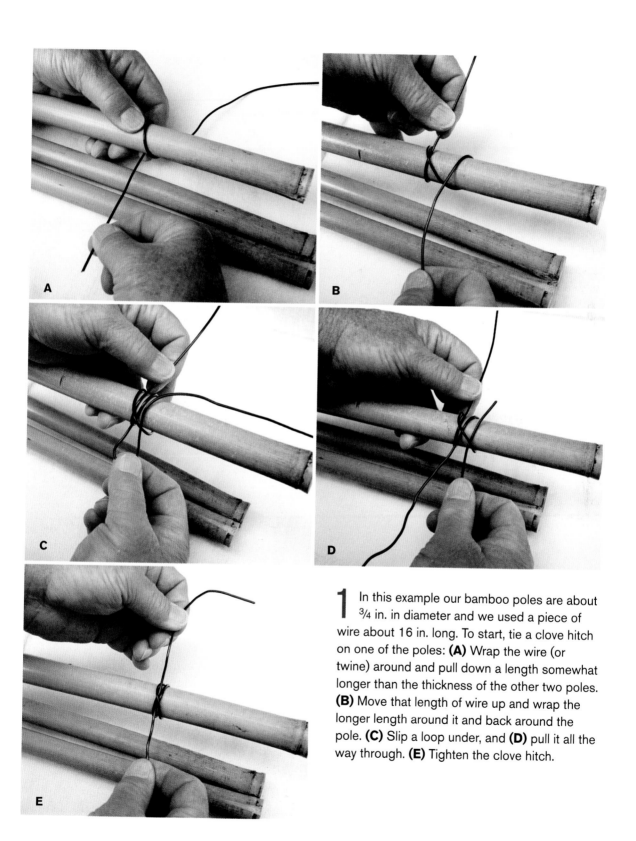

1 In this example our bamboo poles are about
¾ in. in diameter and we used a piece of
wire about 16 in. long. To start, tie a clove hitch
on one of the poles: **(A)** Wrap the wire (or
twine) around and pull down a length somewhat
longer than the thickness of the other two poles.
(B) Move that length of wire up and wrap the
longer length around it and back around the
pole. **(C)** Slip a loop under, and **(D)** pull it all the
way through. **(E)** Tighten the clove hitch.

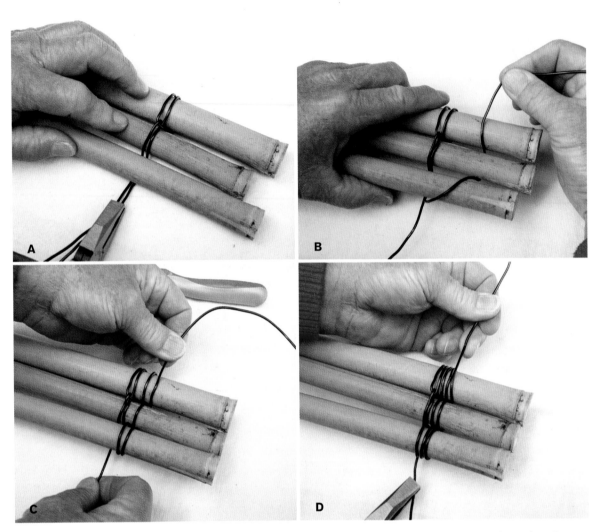

2 Wrap the three poles together. **(A)** Keeping the wires side by side, wrap over one pole and under another. **(B)** Wrap in the other direction with the longer length only. **(C)** Continue wrapping, taking care not to cross over. **(D)** Once you've wrapped three or four times, pull tight using lineman's pliers.

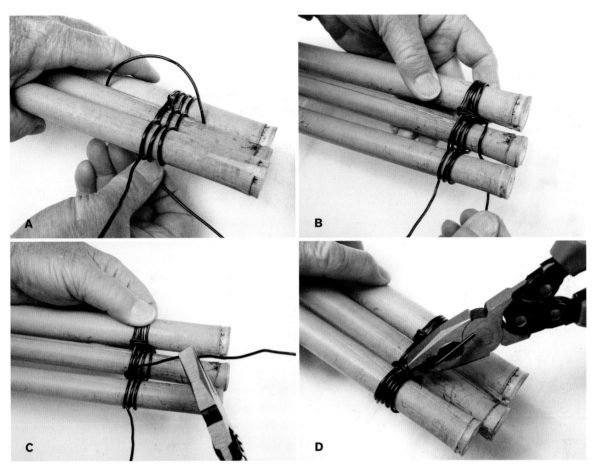

3 It's time for frapping. **(A)** Loop the wire sideways. **(B)** Wrap it sideways two or three times, pull tight, and wrap over to the other pole. **(C)** Wrap sideways again, and pull tight. **(D)** Finish by twisting tight, then cut the loose ends.

4 The three poles now are tied fast, but in a flexible way, so you can open them up.

Bamboo Fan Trellis

This is another quick and easy project that will almost certainly be admired and enjoyed. To add instant visual interest to the trellis, include crooked bamboo for some of the thin crosspieces. This trellis can be anchored to the ground, tied to a tree, or simply leaned in place.

In this project we fasten with both screws and bonsai wire for the verticals and the main horizontals, and we also fasten with only wire for the thin crosspieces, but you can probably get away with only wire for all of the joints.

MATERIALS

- [ ] bamboo poles in three thicknesses: one at 1 in. to 1½ in., five at ¾ in., and two slender poles

- [ ] stainless-steel screws

- [ ] bonsai wire or twine

TOOLS

- [ ] ratcheting garden shears or handsaw

- [ ] drill with screwdriver bit

- [ ] large square

- [ ] lineman's pliers

tip

You are usually working upside-down on this trellis, so every once in a while lift it up to see how it looks on the side that will show.

1 Cut ¾-in. bamboo for the verticals to the desired trellis height. Ratcheting garden shears work well for this or you can use a hand-saw. Arrange the verticals on a flat surface as you like them, and measure the 1-in. to 1½-in. bamboo for the horizontals, they should run past the verticals by a couple of inches on each side.

2 Drill pilot holes and then drive screws to attach the lower horizontal piece; see p. 147 for full instructions. Before drilling pilot holes in the upper horizontal, use a large square to check that it is square to the middle vertical piece.

3 Wrap the screwed joints with wire or twine. Make a simple wrapping that is consistent for each joint. From the slender poles cut, lay out, and tie the small horizontals. Here we've used a crisscrossing pattern, then frapped it (wrapped sideways) for extra tightening (see p. 155). Twist with pliers at the back, and snip off the excess wire with the cutting part of the lineman's pliers.

Bamboo Arbor

This arbor can span a path, a chair, or a collection of potted plants, or it can just sit in the garden beckoning people toward the view. It is definitely a decorative rather than a structural element: It won't be strong enough for kids to climb on, but you can let vines clamber all over it if you like, and it will last for a good many years if unmolested.

The only poles that reach across a horizontal span of any length are the beams, so we've made them of thick 3-in. bamboo; smaller poles might sag over time. All the other pieces are sized for appearance. A variety of sizes are used in symmetrical fashion. If you like, use thicker poles for a more substantial look.

MATERIALS

- □ bamboo poles, 8 ft. long, of various thickness: one at 3 in., four at 2 in., two at 1½ in., two at 1 in., two at ¾ in., and two at ½ in.

- □ stainless-steel screws

- □ bonsai wire or twine

- □ ⅜-in. hardwood dowel, 4 ft. in length

TOOLS

- □ saw

- □ large square

- □ drill with screwdriver bit and Forstner bit

- □ hammer

- □ clamps (optional)

- □ rasp and utility knife

- □ circular saw

- □ ratcheting garden shears, or loppers

BAMBOO ARBOR

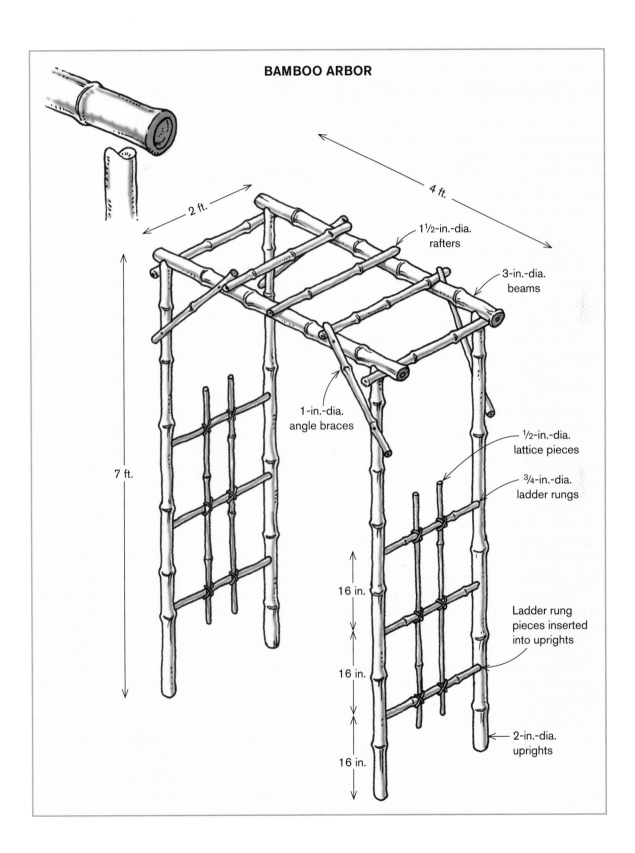

4 ft.

2 ft.

1½-in.-dia. rafters

3-in.-dia. beams

1-in.-dia. angle braces

½-in.-dia. lattice pieces

¾-in.-dia. ladder rungs

Ladder rung pieces inserted into uprights

2-in.-dia. uprights

7 ft.

16 in.

16 in.

16 in.

1 Cut four 2-in.-thick bamboo poles to 7 ft. long for the uprights. Cut ¾-in. bamboo poles into six 2-ft.-long pieces for the ladder-rung pieces. Lay two uprights next to each other, hold them so they won't roll, and mark for where the rungs will be inserted.

FORSTNER BITS

When drilling holes in bamboo, always use a Forstner bit, which bores a clean hole. A twist or spade bit will create splinters and a rough-looking hole. Have a variety of bit sizes on hand to accommodate various pole thicknesses.

tip

Choose bamboo poles that are as straight as possible. You can build with crooked poles, and it can be charming, but with this project it can be difficult to overcome the resulting differences.

2 Use a Forstner bit to bore the holes in the uprights at the marked locations. Test to see that the ladder rung pieces will fit in the holes. Ideally, they should fit in snugly without having to be forced. If they are loose, that's not a problem; if they are too tight, use a knife or a rasp to enlarge the hole.

3 Tap the rungs into the holes of one upright, using a scrap piece of bamboo as your hammer. Insert the rungs into the other upright and tap the whole ladder together.

tip

The ladder and the other parts of the arbor will be unstable and easily wiggled at first, but will gain strength and rigidity slowly as all the pieces are joined together with screws, pegs, and wire.

5 You could use a large clamp or two to hold the pieces together. Here's another, traditional method: Tie with bonsai wire as tightly as you can by hand. Then push or tap the wire at an angle to more firmly clamp the pieces together.

4 Check the ladder for square. Here and throughout construction, check at various points and don't expect perfection; the average of the three rungs should be close to square.

tip

Fastening with hardwood dowels (as in step 6) is a sort of compromise technique. If you want to be more authentic, cut bamboo slats, then use a knife to fashion your own dowels.

6 Use a handsaw to cut a number of hardwood dowels a little shorter than the thickness of the pole you will be joining. With a Forstner bit drill a ⅜-in. hole through the upright and most of the way through the rung piece. Drill the hole about ⅜ in. away from the hole where the rung is inserted and at a slight angle. Use a hammer to tap in a dowel. You could cut the dowel flush, or just leave it protruding out a bit.

7 From the 3-in.-thick bamboo pole cut two 4-ft.-long pieces for the beams. The beams rest on top of the uprights, so the tops of the uprights (that is, the tops of the ladder sections) need to be curve-cut for a neat joint. Hold the end of the upright against a beam and mark for the curve. Cut carefully with a circular saw, slowly eating away at the bamboo until you've come close to finishing the curve cut.

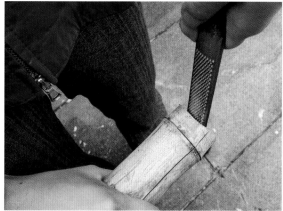

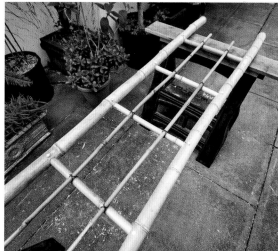

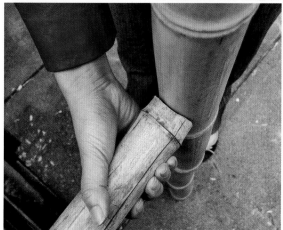

8 Test the fit; it probably won't be ready for prime time. Use a rasp to fine-tune the curve until it fits snugly (though probably not perfectly, but that's OK) against the beam.

9 From the 1/2-in poles cut four 42-in.-long pieces for the lattice, and attach with bonsai wire. A simple crisscrossed wrap is fine, though you may want to tie a frapped joint (see p. 155).

10 From the 1½-in.-thick bamboo poles cut five 30-in.-long pieces for the rafters. Three of these rafters will go on top of the beams, but two will be attached to the top of the ladder uprights, just under the beams. Hold the upright and the rafter in position and drill a pilot hole through the rafter and through just one side of the upright. Drive screws to attach them together.

11 Position the ladder assemblies and the beams together. At each joint, drill a pilot hole and then drive a long screw down through the top of the beam and into the rafter.

12 Space the three middle rafters evenly along the beams. Drill pilot holes, then drive screws down through the rafters into the beams to attach.

13 Check that the arbor is basically square. Out of a 1-in. bamboo pole cut four angle braces. Use the assembled arbor to determine the length. Attach the braces to the beams and the uprights by drilling pilot holes and then driving screws. You may choose to wrap these joints with bonsai wire or twine.

Bamboo Planter

This small decorative feature can be used as a planter, a vase, or a holder of small garden tools or other objects of interest. Skilled artisans may be able to wrap the pieces firmly, but most of us need more help in the form of adhesive or screws, or both.

MATERIALS

- 3-in.-thick or larger bamboo; a 4-ft.-long piece is plenty

- palm rope or other twine

- polyurethane glue or epoxy adhesive

- stainless-steel screws

TOOLS

- handsaw, circular saw, or power miter saw

- rasp

- drill with screwdriver bit

1 Palm rope and other types of twine, if soaked, will tighten when they dry. Soak the twine overnight.

2 Use a saw to cut the bamboo to various lengths so at the bottom there are culms (the bottoms of the bamboo nodules, the only place where the bamboo is not hollow). If you will use this as a planter, drill drainage holes through the bottom culms.

3 Arrange the pieces as you like. You may need to recut some bottoms for stability. Where a culm's outer protrusion meets another piece it may help to file with a rasp for a more even fit.

4 Wrap the first piece with a clove hitch (see p. 153), and tighten.

5 Wrap the twine around the other pieces, taking care not to cross over. Cut very short pieces of bamboo to use as shims and insert them where needed. Apply polyurethane glue for additional strength. If it's still wobbly, drill pilot holes and drive stainless-steel screws.

6 garden projects

STRUCTURES MADE to enhance the garden or landscape are often rough looking, in part because they serve functional purposes but also because they weather the abuses of Mother Nature. Nevertheless, they need not be ratty-looking. For only a little more in the way of materials cost and labor, even a lowly compost bin system can have a bit of style; it won't be the most artistic feature in your landscape, but it can have a humble charm that contributes to the overall design of your space.

Raised Bed

A raised bed lifts the soil up to a more manageable height and, if designed right, can be an interesting design feature in your yard. Because its main purpose is to put flowers, vegetables, or herbs on more prominent display, most raised beds are straightforward in design, taking a back seat to the foliage.

Gardening practicalities: To easily reach the center for weeding and planting, a bed should be no wider than 6 ft. if you have access to both sides and no wider than 3 ft. if you can garden only from one side. (Subtract a foot from those dimensions for people with less than perfect joints and muscles.) If the bed is raised to 16 in. to 24 in. high, you can comfortably kneel beside it. If the bed's structure is fairly wide, you'll be able to comfortably sit on it while tending plants.

This project uses railroad ties, often available at home centers, lumber yards, or recycling centers.

(continued on p. 172)

MATERIALS

- railroad ties, for this project I used six 8-ft.-long ties, 9 in. by 7 in.

- pea gravel

- ⅜-in. reinforcing bar (for a bed that is 8 ft. by 4 ft. you may use as many as twelve 3-ft. sections)

TOOLS

- shovel

- large square

- straight board

- level

- small handsaw for marking

- chisel

- electric or gas chain saw (or make do with a circular saw and reciprocating saw)

- circular saw with metal-cutting blade (or make do with a reciprocating saw with metal-cutting blade)

- drill with long drill bit

- hammer or small sledge hammer

RAISED BED

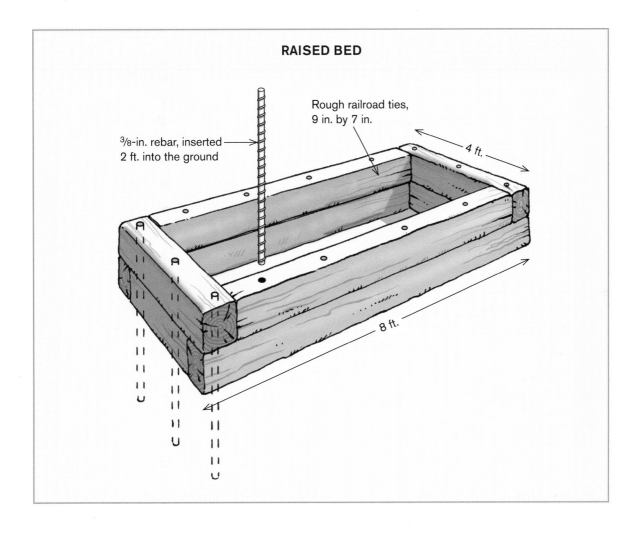

⅜-in. rebar, inserted 2 ft. into the ground

Rough railroad ties, 9 in. by 7 in.

4 ft.

8 ft.

tip

Railroad ties are soaked with creosote as a pest control and preservative measure, and the creosote can leach into plants. You can check out online resources for various ideas about minimizing the effects, but here are some commonly held beliefs: If the ties are old and you do not see or feel liquid creosote, then the possibility of damage to plants is minimal. If creosote does leach into soil, it will most likely not be absorbed by plants' roots. Still, to be safe, keep edible plants at least 6 in. away from the creosoted wood and don't use railroad ties inside greenhouses, because some vapors may be released. If liquid creosote gets on your hands or clothing, the EPA recommends promptly washing it off.

BE SAFE WHEN CUTTING WITH A CHAIN SAW

A chain saw has no guard, so take care to stay out of harm's way. Follow these tips to stay safe:

- Make sure that the chain is sharp and the oil reservoir is full. Check the chain tension as well as its bolts to make sure they are working according to the manufacturer's instructions.

- Place the saw on the ground before starting; don't pull the cord while holding it in the air.

- If you need to refuel a gas-powered saw, see that the saw is cool first. Do not smoke anywhere near it and keep it away from all flames.

- Clear away all debris, dirt, and rocks from the path. Check to be sure you will not cut through a nail or other metal object.

- Do not wear loose-fitting clothes or floppy shirt cuffs. Wear eye protection to protect yourself from flying chips.

- Do not saw with the tip; that can cause kickback.

- Place your body so you will be safe in case of kickback. The photo for step 2, for example, shows kneeling with one leg behind another tie, while the other leg is out of the path of possible kickback.

Sizes vary; ours are about 9 in. tall by 7 in. wide. Quality and appearance also widely vary: Some are in sound shape with only the expected cracks and checks, while others have gaping holes that you may or may not find shabbily attractive. They will be heavy; some can be carried by two hefty guys, while others may need a crew.

1 Determine the size and location of the raised bed. If you will stack the railroad ties, plan to overlap the joints at the corners, as shown in the illustration on p. 171. Use a large square and a handsaw to mark the tie for a square cut. Mark the top of the tie, as well as down the sides.

2 A chain saw is the best tool for this cut. Consult the manufacturer's instructions for safe operation, and make sure the chain is sharp. Kneel or stand above the tie so you can see the downward direction of the cut. Turn the saw on and exert only moderate pressure to make the cut; there is no hurry.

3 If one tie is noticeably wider than the others, you can rip-cut it with a chain saw. The easiest way to do this is with the tie standing upright, as shown. Take your time and cut slowly.

4 Cut lengths of reinforcing bar to fasten the ties together and to the earth. For average soil, the rebar should be driven 16 in. to 25 in. into the ground; for loose, sandy soil, make that 36 in. A circular saw with a metal-cutting blade is the fastest way to cut, and the sparking effects can be fun; just wear goggles to be safe. You can also use a reciprocating saw with a metal-cutting blade, but that will be slow work. Don't try to cut with a hacksaw unless you have lots of time to kill.

tip

If you find yourself going off course while making a chainsaw cut, don't try to make a mid-cut correction; it could cause the saw to bind or kick back dangerously. Instead, turn the saw off, lift it out, and start again.

CUTTING WITH CARPENTRY POWER TOOLS

If you don't have a chain saw, you can cut railroad ties with carpentry tools. The going will be slow; it might take you up to 10 minutes per cut.

First cut all around the tie with a circular saw set for the deepest possible cut. Then use a reciprocating saw with a long pruning blade, which cuts faster than a standard wood-cutting blade, to finish the cut.

5 Excavate for the raised bed. Keep in mind
that 6 in. to 10 in. of soil is plenty deep for
most plants, so the center area can be partly filled
with stone and gravel. Use a shovel to dig a
shallow trench several inches wider than the ties.
Use a straight board to see that the trench is fairly
even. (It does not need to be level—just on an
even plane.)

6 Pour 2 in. to 3 in. of pea gravel into the trench.
Use the straight board to even out the surface,
so the ties will be supported at all points.

7 Set the ties on the gravel. While the ties do not need to be level along their lengths, check that they are at least close to level from side to side. If a tie is out of level, or if it wobbles, roll it over and use the shovel to add or remove gravel as needed to provide a base that supports it at all points.

8 Cut and position ties to form the bed. At the ends the joints should overlap, as shown. If an upper-level tie wobbles, you may need to roll it over and use a hammer and chisel or a saw to remove protrusions from its underside or from the top of the lower-level tie.

9 Continue to adjust and modify the ties as needed so they rest solidly, without wobbling. At the corners and every 2 ft. or so along the lengths of ties use a long drill bit to bore ⅜-in. holes down through both levels of ties.

10 Use a hammer or a small sledge hammer to drive the rebar down through the railroad ties and into the ground. Continue driving until the rebar is flush with the surface of the ties. In time the cut rebar ends will rust attractively. Fill the bed with garden soil or a mixture of topsoil, peat moss, manure, and perhaps composted soil, then plant.

Compost Bin

A compost bin is a sign of a serious gardener, as well as a person who wants to make responsible use of kitchen and lawn waste. Most large containers will work for composting, as long as they encase the material in a way that allows some air flow—but not too much.

How much air flow is best for you depends on your local climate as well as the type of material you will compost. Some gardeners use bins that are entirely made of wire mesh, for plenty of aeration; others prefer to surround compost with nearly solid fencing so the compost can really brew. Check with successful local gardeners to choose the style you prefer. For this project we've taken a middle route: The rear is made of mesh, while the sides are made of boards. You may choose to use more or fewer boards or wire mesh sections. The front has channels in which boards can be slid in or out, depending on the height of the compost.

Some compost bins have a single bin, while others have three; again, we've taken a middle course, with two bins. It would be simple to modify these plans for one or three bins.

Treated lumber is used here, because it will stay rot-free the longest. Most people accept that the newer treatments (since about 2003) are safe, but if you'd prefer you could build with cedar or redwood.

MATERIALS

- six 8-ft. 4×4 pressure-treated posts
- nine 12-ft. pressure-treated 5/4×6 decking boards
- chicken wire or hardware cloth, 3 ft. by 10 ft.
- 2½-in. nails or deck screws
- 1-in. staples for power stapler, or ½-in. staples for hand stapler
- angle square
- post level and carpenter's level
- power nailer, power stapler, or hand stapler
- tin snips (aviation shears)

TOOLS

- framing square
- shovel
- post-hole digger
- mason's line
- framing square
- circular saw

COMPOST BIN

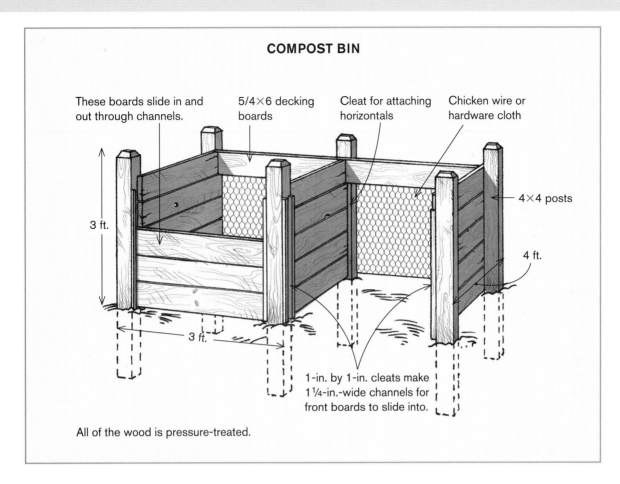

These boards slide in and out through channels.

5/4×6 decking boards

Cleat for attaching horizontals

Chicken wire or hardware cloth

4×4 posts

3 ft.

4 ft.

3 ft.

1-in. by 1-in. cleats make 1¼-in.-wide channels for front boards to slide into.

All of the wood is pressure-treated.

1 Lay out the locations of six posts for two bins that are 3 ft. wide and 4 ft. deep. Drive stakes indicating the centers of the four perimeter post holes and string lines between them. Use a framing square to check that the layout is square. Then drive stakes for the two inside posts.

tip

Another method for installing posts: Dig post holes and install posts that "run wild"—rise up higher than they need to be. Once the posts are set, use a level to mark them for cutting to the same heights. In our plan we first cut decorative post tops, and so need to install the posts at the correct height to begin with.

CUTTING A DECORATIVE POST TOP

You can buy post caps that install on top of straight-cut posts. Or, as we show here, make your own decorative design.

1 Use an angle square to draw two lines around the post near the top: a cut line and a line for the decorative groove.

2 Set a circular saw to cut at a 30-degree bevel. This will produce a post top with a low-sloped point.

3 Using an angle square as a guide, cut along each top line. When you make the last cut, the point will be complete.

4 Set a circular saw blade to cut at a depth of only ¼ in. Cut on one side of the bottom line, then cut the other side, to produce a groove that is about ¼ in. wide.

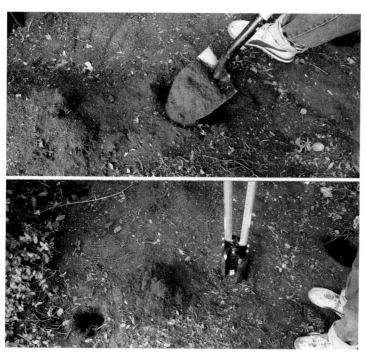

2 Start digging with a shovel to clearly mark the post locations. Dig around each stake, keeping it centered in the hole for as long as possible. Then switch to a post-hole digger. Dig holes at least 2 ft. deep—deeper if the soil is sandy or loose.

3 Set the first post in its hole at the height you want all the posts to be. Put a post level on it and start to fill the hole around it. Tamp the soil, add more, and repeat until the post is firm.

tip

If you run into a root while digging a post hole you may be able to cut it with a shovel or the post-hole digger. If not, a reciprocating saw is often the best tool to use. If the root is very large you may need to move the post (and probably other posts as well), or just live with a post that is not sunk very deep.

4 Set other posts in their holes and check that their tops will be level with your first post. In order to achieve the correct heights you will need to either dig deeper, add soil, or cut a post.

5 Continue installing posts. Use straight boards and a framing square to keep the structure square. Also check that the posts are correctly spaced. On a rough structure like this, things don't need to be perfect; you can usually live with posts that are off by ½ in. or so.

6 The front row of posts is the most visible, so use a straight board to keep the three posts in a straight line. (Here we installed the front center post slightly higher than the others, for a modest decorative flourish.)

7 Cut decking boards to span the posts on one side. In order to leave room for a channel to slide the front boards in and out, attach a temporary cleat to keep the ends of the boards you are installing 2 in. shy of the front of the front post in a straight vertical line.

8 Install decking boards in the same way on the other side, using a temporary cleat to keep them 2 in. shy of the front of the front post. For rigidity, install a single decking board spanning across the top of the back posts.

9 Use tin snips (aviation shears) to cut chicken wire or hardware cloth to span across the back of the composter. Instead of cutting it to height, bend it over and tap with a hammer and block of wood as shown; this will make it stronger.

10 Staple chicken wire to the back of the structure. Use a power nailer with 1-in. staples, as shown. Or use a hand stapler with 1/2-in. staples. After driving them with a stapler, you may need to finish pounding them in using a hammer.

11 Rip-cut pieces of decking to 1 in. wide and use them as cleats for attaching the middle horizontal boards to the centers of the middle posts as you did for the side horizontal boards in step 7. Also attach cleats to the sides of the front middle post, as shown, to create a 1 1/4-in.-wide channel for the front boards to slide in and out of.

12 At the side front posts, install a cleat, as shown, to create a 1 1/4-in.-wide channel between the ends of the horizontal boards and the cleat. Cut front boards that fit loosely so they can be easily slipped in and out as needed.

Potting Table

If you enjoy puttering around in the garden and often find yourself repotting plants or starting plants from seeds, you'll really appreciate the convenience of an organized work table with built-in shelves and space for large bins. A potting table is a gardener's office and a play space all rolled into one.

Look online and you'll see plenty of potting tables for $700 and up; this one costs much less, and has features many of the store-bought versions don't.

There is a hatch on the table that can be removed to reveal a mesh-covered opening. The shelf below is the right height to slide a large plastic bin below

(continued on p. 184)

MATERIALS

- □ six 12-ft. pieces of 5/4×6 decking, for table top, shelf supports, and rear uprights (we used "thick" decking, which is about 1¼ in. thick)

- □ 4 ft. of pressure-treated 2×2

- □ two 12-ft. 1×6s, for shelves

- □ four 12-ft. pressure-treated 2×4s, for table framing

- □ small piece of hardware cloth (wire mesh)

- □ 2-in. and 2½-in. deck screws

- □ 1-in. staples for power stapler, or ½-in. staples for hand stapler

- □ stain and sealer

TOOLS

- □ chopsaw or circular saw
- □ jigsaw
- □ drill with screwdriver bit
- □ router with roundover bit
- □ angle square
- □ framing square
- □ tin snips (aviation shears)
- □ power nailer, power stapler, or hand stapler

POTTING TABLE

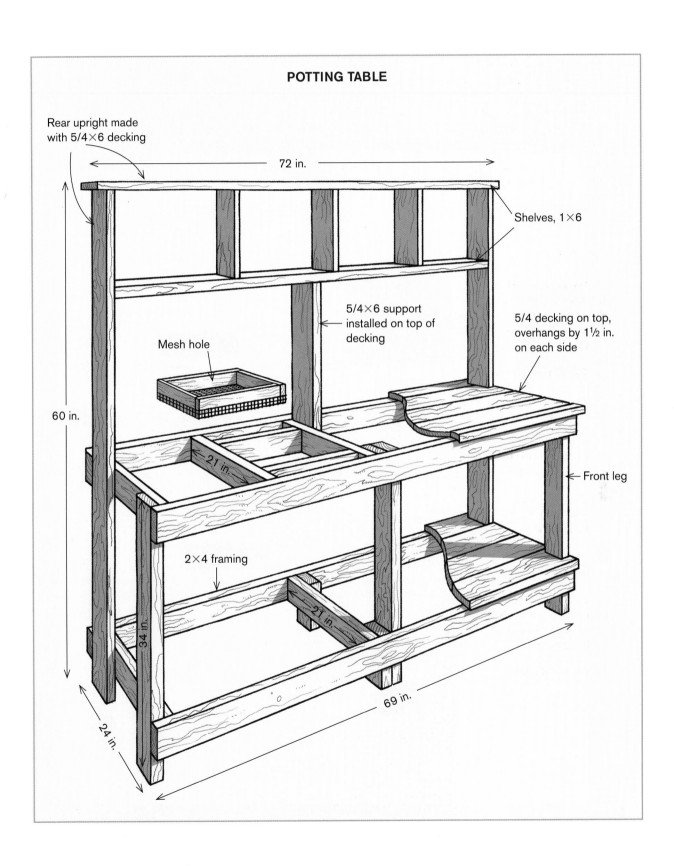

Rear upright made with 5/4×6 decking

72 in.

Shelves, 1×6

5/4×6 support installed on top of decking

5/4 decking on top, overhangs by 1½ in. on each side

Mesh hole

60 in.

21 in.

Front leg

2×4 framing

34 in.

21 in.

24 in.

69 in.

the opening. That means you can easily sweep dirt into the hatch, and the soil will filter down into the bin while any large stones or debris will be caught by the mesh.

This bench is spacious at almost 6 ft. in length and can hold plenty of stuff while also providing space to stretch out for elaborate projects. If space is limited, you may opt instead for a 4-ft.- or 5-ft.-long table. The upper shelves can be easily modified—made taller or shorter, or with more or fewer vertical dividers—you can tailor each section to meet your needs.

1 If your lumber is fairly dry, apply a water-based stain and sealer to the boards ahead of time; that way you need only touch up after construction. If your boards are wet, or if you choose to use an oil or alkyd-based stain, apply only after the wood is dry enough that beads of water soak in. Stack the boards neatly on top of each other and apply stain to the edges; then lay them side by side and apply to the faces. Be vigilant about brushing away unsightly drips; they will be difficult to remove after they dry.

2 Cut the framing boards to the desired dimensions. For this design, cut four pieces 69 in. long from 2×4s and seven pieces 21 in. long from 2×4s; both will be horizontal pieces. Cut the three front legs to 34 in. from a 2×4 and the two rear uprights to 60 in. from 5/4×6 decking.

tip

If you are shorter or taller than average you may choose to raise or lower the table height. If you do that, the front legs will need to be changed accordingly; their length is 1 in. to 1¼ in. below the finished table height (depending on the thickness of the decking used for the table top).

3 Lay out for where the long 2×4 horizontals will attach to the rear vertical uprights (which are 5/4×6). Here, the lower 2×4 will be installed with its top 7 in. from the bottom, meaning the bottom shelf will be 8 in. or so above the ground; you may choose to lower or raise this. The upper 2×4 will be installed with its top 34 in. from the bottom, so the table will be 35 in. or so above the ground.

4 Attach the rear horizontal 2×4s between the rear uprights. Place each horizontal against the decking board (on the locations marked in step 3) and drive 2½-in. screws to attach.

5 Lay the two long front horizontals on a table and mark them for the locations of the three front legs (using the same guidelines as in step 3). Transfer the marks to the edges so you can see their positions when you build (next step).

6 Attach the long horizontals to the three front legs using the lines you drew in the previous step. Check the structure for square, and adjust as needed. Drive two 2½-in. screws into each joint.

7 Attach the short (21-in.) horizontals to the legs. (You are building with the structure on its side, so at this point the horizontals are vertical.) Check each for square, then drive two 2½-in. screws into each joint.

8 Now assemble the basic frame: Stand the rear assembly (which you built in step 4) upright. Position the front assembly (which you built in steps 6 and 7) against it and check the whole assembly for square. Drive screws to attach the front assembly to the rear assembly.

9 Determine the size you want the hatch opening to be and install a horizontal 2×4 for its outside frame.

10 Cut and install the rearmost decking board between the rear uprights, overhanging the framing by 1½ in. or so. (Because there is a pipe on this wall, we chose to overhang the rear board by 2¼ in. so the table would go up against the wall and we wouldn't have to cut a notch for the pipe.) Measure the total width of the table top; you'll probably need to rip-cut one piece to get the total width that you want. Make the rip-cut and rout the cut edge with a roundover bit to mimic the factory-rounded decking edge.

11 To notch around the rear upright, hold the board in place, overhanging the framing by 1½ in., and use a tape measure and angle square to mark for the notch. Cut first with a circular saw, taking care not to go too far. Then finish the cut using a jigsaw.

12 Build a simple 2×2 frame for the hatch. Make it ¼ in. narrower than the opening you made in step 9, to allow room for the wire mesh.

13 Use tin snips (aviation shears) to cut the wire mesh 2 in. wider and longer than the frame. Snip at the corners so you can bend the mesh there.

14 Bend the mesh so it molds against the outside of the frame. Tap with a hammer and scrap of wood first, then remove the frame and bend a bit more. Set the frame back in place, and drive ½-in. staples into every other wire. If the staples do not go all the way in, tap with a hammer. (If you have a power stapler, use it with 1-in. staples, for a stronger hold.)

15 Position the screened frame flush with the top of the framing and drive 2½-in. screws on each side to attach.

16 Install the decking for the table top so it overhangs 1½ in. on each side. Where the decking meets the hatch, have it slightly overhang the screen's frame on each side so the hatch will have something to rest on. At the front and back the decking can completely cover the screen framing.

17 Build a simple hatch out of full-width and half-width decking boards. It should be ⅛ in. shorter than the opening along the length of the decking and ¼ in. shorter on the other edges so you can easily lift it up.

tip

For this project we butted the upper decking boards tightly together, for a more table-like surface. On the lower shelf we left gaps so debris can fall through easily. In time most decking boards will shrink slightly, producing small gaps.

18 Install the lower decking boards to make a large shelf for bins. Use only four full-width boards and install with gaps between them. You will need to add a short 2×4 piece to support the decking on one side of the center leg.

19 Cut a 1×6 to 72 in. and screw it to the top of the rear uprights so it overhangs 1½ in. on each side. Cut a lower shelf from 1×6 to fit between the uprights. Install it at the height of your choosing, checking for square, and driving three 2-in. screws into each joint.

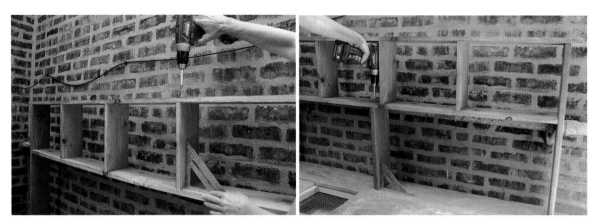

20 Cut dividers out of a 1×6 and install them between the two shelves to create cubbies of a convenient size. Check each for square as you drive screws to attach. Also install an upright shelf support near the middle of the table to keep the shelves from sagging.

21 Touch up the stain and sealer as needed. Allow the sealer several days to completely dry before using the table.

Strawberry Pyramid

This pyramid is an elegant way to produce a plethora of delicious fruit. If you plant everbearing strawberries, you'll be gathering berries all summer long and into the fall. Of course, you can also plant flowers or herbs.

A classic strawberry pyramid rests on the ground, and you can certainly build this project that way. We've added a plywood bottom and casters so the pyramid can be moved around on a deck or patio. Serious fruit-growers may want to rotate the

(continued on p. 192)

MATERIALS

- ☐ 3-ft. cedar 2×2
- ☐ four 8-ft. 5/4×6 cedar decking boards
- ☐ ½-in. pressure-treated plywood, about 2 ft. square
- ☐ four casters
- ☐ 1⅝-in. deck screws
- ☐ polyurethane construction adhesive, with caulk gun
- ☐ stain and sealer
- ☐ soil mix
- ☐ strawberries or other plants

TOOLS

- ☐ tablesaw or circular saw
- ☐ compound miter chopsaw (or make do with a circular saw and large angle square)
- ☐ router with roundover bit
- ☐ framing square and angle square
- ☐ long clamp
- ☐ drill with screwdriver bit and pilot/counterbore bit

pyramid every few days so all sides get enough sun to produce fruit.

There are several odd angles in this project. Our instructions will tell you the basic angles for setting your saws and cutlines, but because saw guides and angle settings are not perfect you will likely need to make small adjustments and fine-tune the angles as you work. Expect to spend some time, but not too much time, finagling.

A compound-miter chopsaw is the best tool to use, but cutting these angles with a circular saw is surprisingly doable if you have good cutting skills. A chopsaw that is not made for compound miters will not help with this job.

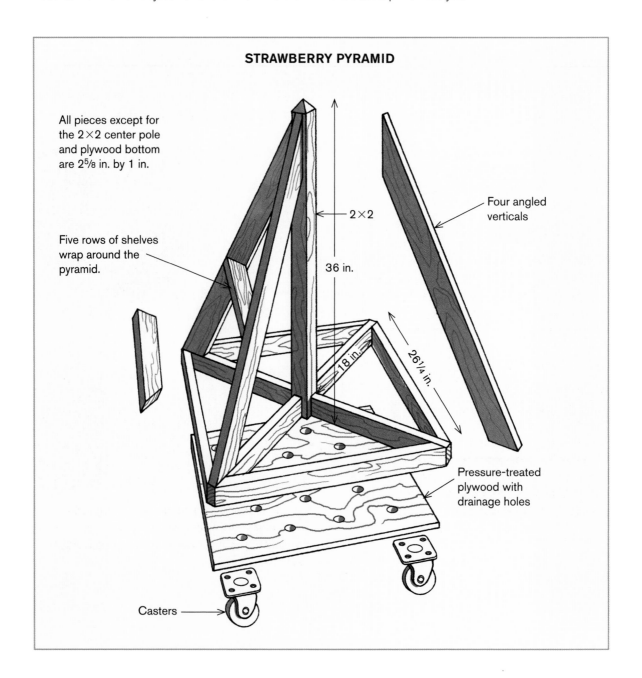

STRAWBERRY PYRAMID

All pieces except for the 2×2 center pole and plywood bottom are 2⅝ in. by 1 in.

Five rows of shelves wrap around the pyramid.

2×2

36 in.

18 in.

26¼ in.

Four angled verticals

Pressure-treated plywood with drainage holes

Casters

1 Cut a 2×2 to 36 in. Use a square to draw a line around it about ¾ in. from the top. Set a chop-saw to cut at a 30-degree angle and cut along the lines to produce a low-sloping point.

2 Use a tablesaw or a circular saw with a rip guide to rip-cut decking boards in half; they will be about 2⅝ in. wide. Aside from the center 2×2 pole and the plywood bottom, the entire pyramid will be built with these boards.

3 Cut four radiating pieces 18 in. long, with straight cuts. Use a pilot/counterbore bit to drill angled pilot holes at one end on both sides (see next step).

4 Apply a dab of polyurethane construction adhesive to the pilot-hole-drilled end of each piece. Use a long clamp to hold each piece in position in a radiating fashion, as shown. Drive screws through the tops to attach all four. Then turn the structure over and drive screws through the bottoms.

5 Cut four perimeter pieces with 45-degree bevels at each end; make them 26¼ in. long. Attach by drilling pilot holes and driving screws that reach through the radiating pieces as well as the adjoining perimeter piece.

tip

Dry-fit the four pieces before applying adhesive and driving screws. If the last piece is too long, avoid the temptation to cut only that piece; doing so will destroy the symmetry, meaning the angles will change for many other pieces. Instead, use a square as shown to determine how overlong the piece is. Divide that number by four, disassemble the other pieces, and cut all four pieces to the same dimension.

6 To mark for cutting the angles on the angled verticals, clamp a board in position. Its top should be in line with the pointed cut at the top, and its bottom should be in line with the outside corner. Use a straightedge to check alignment.

8 Measure for the length of the angled vertical. Use the angles captured in step 7 to mark for cuts on both ends. Make the cuts with a circular saw. Cut another piece at the same length and angle.

7 Holding the piece in place, use a straightedge to mark a line parallel to the radiating piece at the bottom. Also mark for the angle at the top. Do this on the other side as well (because the pole may not be sticking straight up), and if the angles differ, split the difference.

9 Hold the two pieces on each side in position (with the rounded edges facing outward) and check for a tight fit. It is likely that you will need to mark the board on one end to micro-adjust the angle.

10 Once you are happy with the angle and length, use the first piece as a template for marking the others. Drill angled pilot/counterbore holes at both ends.

11 Dry-fit the pieces to be sure they will fit correctly. Apply adhesive to both ends of the angled verticals and attach all four with screws at both ends.

tip -

The pieces should fit fairly well, with no variations of fit greater than ¼ in. To correct boards that are slightly long at the top, knock them down a bit using a belt sander.

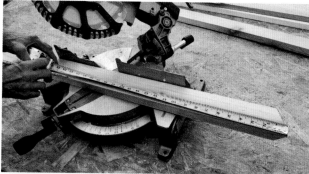

12 Now it's time to cut the shelves at compound angles. If you have a compound-miter saw, set the angle or miter (the angle of the cut in relation to the vertical fence) at 26 degrees. Then set the bevel (the angle of the sawblade in relation to the horizontal base) at 41 degrees.

13 Cut the compound miter at one end. Flip the board over, reverse it end to end, and measure 18 in. from the outside tip of the first cut to mark the outside tip of the other cut. To make this second cut, sight along the blade as shown.

14 Test the fit. The board should rest flat against the angled uprights on both sides while it is exactly parallel with the bottom perimeter board. Check at all four places to be sure. If the fit or length is not right, recut and retry as needed. (You can use leftover pieces for future, shorter shelves.)

15 Once you are happy with the fit, use the first piece as a template to mark and cut the other three.

CUTTING SHELVES WITH A CIRCULAR SAW

You can cut the compound angles for the shelves with a circular saw as long as you have good skills and some patience. Set the circular saw's bevel to 41 degrees. Use a large angle square to mark the board for a cut at 26 degrees. (To make it easy to find this angle, we have drawn a pencil line on the square at the 26 mark.) Hold the saw's baseplate flat on the board as you make the cut. Measure and make the other cut. Test the fit; you will likely need to make a minor adjustment or two.

16 For these and all the other shelves, use a router with a roundover bit to round over all the long rip-cut sides (but not the miter-and-bevel-cut ends).

17 Drill pilot/counterbore holes at angles as shown near the ends of the shelves. Attach by applying adhesive to the ends, then driving screws into the angled uprights.

18 To cut shelves for the next four rows, use the same angle and bevel. Make the shelves for each row 2 in. shorter than the last. (The bottom row shelves are 18 in. long, the next row is 16 in. long, the next is 14 in. long, then 12 in. long, and finally, 10 in. long.) Attach in the same way.

19 If you choose to stain and seal the pyramid, tip it on its side and apply to as much as you can reach; then tip and apply again, and so on.

20 Cut a sheet of pressure-treated plywood ½ in. smaller than the bottom of the pyramid. Attach with screws and drill a series of drainage holes. At each corner attach a caster with four screws.

21 For a good strawberry medium, add some sand to potting soil. Pour into the pyramid directly from the bag and use a trowel to move the dirt around. Insert small strawberry plants, spaced 6 in. to 8 in. apart.

index

If you like this book, you'll love *Fine Woodworking*.

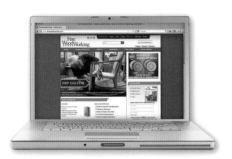